SICILY

An Informal History

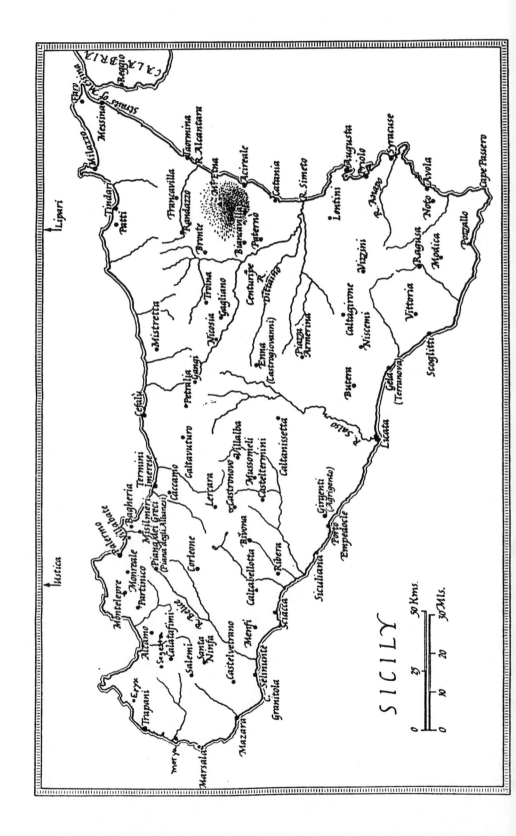

SICILY

50 Kms.

30 Mls.

SICILY

An Informal History

PETER SAMMARTINO
WILLIAM ROBERTS

New York • Toronto • London
Cornwall Books

© 1992 by
Rosemont Publishing & Printing Corporation

Cornwall Books
440 Forsgate Drive
Cranbury, New Jersey 08512

Cornwall Books
25 Sicilian Avenue
London WC1A 2QH, England

Cornwall Books
P. O. Box 39, Clarkson Pstl. Stn.
Mississauga, ONT., Canada L5J 3X9

Library of Congress Cataloging-in-Publication Data

Sammartino, Peter.
    Sicily : an informal history / Peter Sammartino, William
Roberts.
        p.   cm.
    ISBN 0-8453-4843-4 (alk. paper)
    1. Sicily (Italy)—History.   I. Roberts, William, 1945–
II. Title.
    DG866.S225   1992
    945'.8—dc20   92-1374
                                                        CIP

PRINTED IN THE UNITED STATES OF AMERICA

To Sally

Acknowledgments

IT WAS PETER SAMMARTINO'S DEAREST WISH TO SEE THIS WORK COMpleted. He considered it to be one of the most important projects of his later years. It is in fact, the culmination of many years of research on the fascinating and important history of Sicily. When he asked me to join him in this endeavor, I was both honored and intrigued at the prospect and soon, many pleasant days would be spent in collaboration.

In dedicating this book to Sally Sammartino we especially wanted to acknowledge the debt of gratitude owed to someone who had been a constant source of inspiration and encouragement. She was with us every step of the way. Now hopefully, this completed history will serve as a tribute to them both.

Also, thanks are due to the staffs of Fairleigh Dickinson University Library, the New York Public Library, the Italian Cultural Institute of New York, and Cornwall Books for their kind assistance, and to the many family members, friends, and colleagues, in particular Marie and Sal Guerra, Elizabeth, William, and Lisa Roberts, Julia Scaramelli, Sr. Margherita Marchione M.P.F., Dr. Heinz Mackensen, Dean Kenneth T. Vehrkens, Jeannette Schuffenhauer, Irma Sullivan, and Kathy Falcicchio all of whom gave enthusiastic support to our efforts.

W.R.

Table of Contents

Introduction

EW ISLANDS HAVE PLAYED SUCH A SIGNIFICANT ROLE OVER SUCH A long period of time as Sicily. Although relatively small—just under 10,000 square miles—less than a third of the size of Ireland and a fourth of the size of Cuba—Sicily has an unparalleled location. Only two miles separate it from the Italian mainland at Messina and the shortest distance to Africa is less than 100 miles. It has therefore been both a gateway and crossroads, dividing the Mediterrean into eastern and western halves and serving as a link between Europe and Africa. In fact, one of the ancient names for Sicily, "Trinacria," reflects the triangular shape of the island with important headlands at each point. The island was a meeting place as well as a battleground, and its size and the productivity of its soil raised Sicily beyond the position of a mere trading post or stopover, and attracted conquerers and migrants. On the other hand, Sicily was not large enough to be a threat to more powerful neighbors in Europe and Africa nor strong enough to retain its independence against greater powers such as Rome or Spain.

These factors determined Sicilian history. The list of migrants and conquerors is long and includes unnamed prehistoric peoples, the Sicani, Sicels, and Elymians, Greeks and Carthaginians, Romans, Jews, Vandals, Saracens, Normans, Spaniards, and others.

What drew many of these peoples was the renowned fertility and productivity of the island. The Greek philosopher Strabo wrote in the 1st century A.D. "as for the goodness of the land, why should I speak of it when it is talked about by everyone?" Ancient Sicily was a land that produced cereals, olives, wine and fruits, and held vast forests of chestnut, pine, and fir. It was these factors which must have attracted the first settlers to the island—a process which has continued throughout her long and varied history.

SICILY

An Informal History

I
Beginnings

(PRE-GREEK PERIOD)

WE KNOW AS MUCH ABOUT THE BEGINNINGS OF SICILY AS WE KNOW about the beginnings of our own country before it was settled and colonized. Probably, at the beginning, there were no inhabitants on the island, the earliest migrants coming by sea, since a land bridge between Sicily and Italy or North Africa never existed. These earliest inhabitants came during the Advanced Palaeolithic Period, sometime before 20,000 B.C. Evidence of Old Stone Age habitation, in caves and cliff shelters, is found in areas along the north coast, in the southeast, and the west. Stone tools and cave paintings link these cultures to those of western Europe of the same period. On the Egadi Islands of Favignana, Marettimo, and Levanzo, off Sicily's western coast, prehistoric man left his mark incised or painted on the walls of caves. These images, that can be seen today, depict red deer, oxen, and small horses and there is a particularly lively figure of a young doe, turning its head—surely one of the most beautiful expressions of prehistoric art in Sicily. There are also humans portrayed, and these naturalistic human and animal images resemble those found in Spain and France done during the same period.

Palaeolithic life on Sicily continued unchanged for thousands of years until the island became part of a general transformation that was taking place sometime before 3,000 B.C. in other parts of the Mediterranean. This was the emergence of peasant communities in the Neolithic Age. These new communities all practiced agriculture, the domestication of animals, and the manufacture of pottery. The most important example of this Neolithic culture on Sicily is known as the Stentinello culture, after a village near Syracuse where it was first identified. It was located in eastern Sicily and evidence of it has been found also on the northeast island of Lipari. About 3,000 B.C.

13

the Stentinello culture adopted metallurgy (in this case, the use of copper) and began the practice of carving out chamber tombs from rock. Before this time, graves had been shallow ditches or enclosures dug in the ground. This new "oven-shaped tomb," or "tombe a forno," became common throughout Sicily during the prehistoric period and remained in use until after the coming of the Greeks. Also, on the island of Pantelleria there dates, from this time, the curious stone structures known as "Sesi." Built over five thousand years ago, these funereal monuments were apparently also used for divination. The culture that produced them has, of course, long since vanished, but has left besides the "sesi," traces of their existence in various boundary walls that were built to defend the villages. For all of Europe this period, the Copper Age, was itself a prelude to the Bronze Age, and with it the appearance in Sicily of three distinct pre-Greek peoples: the Sicani, the Sicels, and the Elymians.

The Sicani probably came from the Iberian peninsula and settled quite naturally on the west coast of the island. They were followed by the Sicels from the Italian mainland who settled in the east while the Elymians settled in the northwestern part of the island. This last group in time developed centers at Segesta, Halicyae (Salemi), and Eryx (present day Erice), where they had an urban existence resembling that of the later Greeks. Definite examples of these three early peoples exist from the time of the late Bronze Age (about 1200 B.C.), a period of extensive movement, migration, and disturbance in the Mediterranean area. There is proof of these waves of migration into Sicily. The earliest evidence of the Sicels, who gave their name to the island, is found in hewn chambers, some found containing squatting skeletons, and in examples of pottery. Archeology also allows us to be fairly sure that the Elymians were responsible for the origin of the towns of Segesta and Erice. Today, one can visit a Bronze Age site at Castelluccio, near Noto. An entire village of that era has been unearthed and has given its name to a prehistoric period, the "Castelluccian." The round mud huts of that culture can be seen and, on a nearby rocky slope, can be found a huge necropolis consisting of 200 small man-made caves which were used as sepulchers. The vestibules were open and the entrance was closed with slabs of stone decorated with spiral patterns. The dead were buried here in a crouched position to make best use of the narrow space and to make room for the burial of relatives or neighbors. But, beyond such examples and what the Greek sources tell us of these peoples (and these are often sketchy and contradictory), we know little.

Nonetheless, the contributions of these pre-Greek peoples were important. They did, of course, make possible an easier settlement for the Greeks by clearing land and beginning cultivation on the island. Later, they would intermarry with the early Greek colonizers. And, in certain instances, aspects of the religious cults of these early peoples were adopted by the Greeks and merged with their own. For example, the Greeks, who, like the earliest inhabitants of Sicily, worshiped natural powers, took over a cult of the Palaci, a branch of the Sicel people, that was centered in an extinct volcano 25 miles west of Catania. The Greeks converted this site into a center of worship of the sons of Zeus and maintained there the ancient tradition that anyone who swore a false oath at the shrine would be cursed. But, aside from such instances, the role of the pre-Greek peoples would soon be overshadowed. During the late Iron Age, about 750 B.C., while these early tribes were attempting to extend their own control over the island, two important colonizations began: that of the Phoenicians or Carthaginians, and the Greeks. The coming of these later peoples marked the beginnings of recorded history in Sicily and brought about an important change in the development of the island.

II

The Greeks

COLONIZATION AND MOVEMENT OF POPULATIONS WAS ALWAYS A feature of Greek life, and the colonization of Sicily was just such an enterprise, but on a grand scale. Agriculturally, Greece was a relatively poor country. Land was always limited and, because the ancient Greek culture emphasized inheritance by a single heir, additional offspring were often disinherited. Thus, they had to seek land elsewhere. Many would leave the Greek homeland for other regions of the Mediterranean. With this there was, too, a personal element. A general spirit of adventure, characteristic of the age and similar to the times of the Portuguese and Spanish explorations or of the American pioneering of the nineteenth century, impelled many in the ancient Greek world, especially the young, to seek new trade, territories, and experiences. Sicily, for these ancient adventurers, offered such an opportunity. The island has, in fact, been referred to by modern scholars as *" 'quest'America dell'antichità"*—"this America of antiquity." There, the verdant spring and dusty, arid summers offered, with its Mediterranean landscape, an environment that was already familiar to the Greeks.

To further understand this phenomenon of the Greek overseas colonies, it is first necessary to define the word "colonization" in relation to Hellenic culture. The phrase can be misleading in terms of what actually happened. Unlike colonies established in modern times, the colonies of the Greeks were considered to be independent immediately upon their founding. They became separate communities with only a spiritual tie to the "metropolis," or "mother-city," and had self-rule. They were never subject states. Of course, when the Greeks came to an area such as Sicily, the original inhabitants were pushed to the interior. There were some attempts, especially by the Sicels to re-establish themselves—the most famous being the

16

movement started by the Sicel leader Ducetius in 450 B.C.—but these efforts were not successful. Many were absorbed by the new immigrants, especially through intermarriage, and their cultures soon merged with the Greek.

From the map it is clear that the Greeks would inevitably arrive at Sicily—and quite naturally on the eastern coast. Even in the poet Homer's time, before the eighth century B.C., there was a detailed knowledge of Sicily. That poet, in his epic, the "Odyssey," noted that when the Greeks arrived in Sicily they found the island lush with woodlands and vineyards. And, in the same work, the rocks of Scylla and Charybdis on either side of the Straits of Messina that divide Sicily from the mainland, are described as a roaring marine monster and a beautiful woman who draw sailors to their death. Just beyond present day Catania can be seen the seven *Isole dei Ciclopi* ("islands of the Cyclops"), also known as the Faraglioni, which the Greeks said were the rocks that the Cyclops hurled at Odysseus's ship. In the *Odyssey* are also described the Aeolian, or Lipari, islands which the Greeks believed included a "floating island," Aeolia, home of the wind god Aeolus. Even in prehistoric times, people had migrated to these islands of the north coast of Sicily in search of obsidian, the black volcanic glass used for weapons and implements. Perhaps best known today of the seven Aeolian islands is Stromboli, whose peak is still volcanicly active.

As a seafaring people, the Greeks did, of course, try to explore a little further west each time. Settlers from Corinth in Greece founded Syracuse, and around 729 B.C. other Greek colonies were established in Leontini, Catania, and Zankle (now Messina). The name Zankle was derived from the *Sicel* "sickle" and describes the shape of its harbor. Often, inhabitants of a colony would themselves branch off and start a new city. It was settlers from Syracuse, for example, who established Kamarina in 600 B.C. In this sense, the Sicilian colonies can be divided into two groups—primary colonies established directly from Greece and secondary colonies founded as offshoots of these. In some cases the offshoots eclipsed the parent colonies just as Syracuse surpassed its mother-city back in Greece. Again, it was the lack of land or fear of overpopulation that provided the incentive to found these new cities. A further example is Naxos, founded in 734 B.C. by the Greeks from Euboea. Settlers from Naxos in turn founded Cumae near what is today Naples. The Greeks also settled on the western coast of Italy because of its proximity to important metal deposits. In doing so they entered into rivalry with the Etruscans, a people of northern and central Italy, and that is one of the reasons the Greeks didn't colonize further up on the Italian coast.

As time went on, the Greeks became more adventurous in exploring Sicily. They went along the southern shore and in 688 B.C. founded Gela and, in 628 B.C., Selinus and Akragas (now Agrigento) which was described by the Greek poet Pindar as "the fairest city of mortal men." Settlers from the Greek island of Rhodes were especially prominent in colonizing this area. The Greeks also founded a colony on the northern shore, Himera. Settlements were also established inland. Because they had the custom of beaching, not anchoring their ships, the Greeks were not concerned about the need for a deep harbor, although there is one at Syracuse. Gela and Agrigento are examples of cities built inland. Of course, once established, the Greek cities in Sicily developed their own commercial activities. They were never mere trading-posts and were chiefly concerned with their own interests rather than those of the mother-cities. In time, Sicily would be called *Magna Graecia* or "Greater Greece" and would contain some of the largest cities of the Greek world. In fact, two of the three largest cities of the ancient Greek world, Syracuse and Agrigento, were found in Sicily. They each had more than 20,000 citizens and were rivaled only by Athens. Finally, in 396 B.C., the last Greek colony on the island, Tyndaris, was founded by the tyrant Dionysos I (it was later destroyed by the Saracens, but the ruins can still be seen today).

But, at the same time as the early Greek colonization of the island was taking place, another people, the Carthaginians, were also establishing commercial enclaves there. Inevitably, there would be conflict between the two groups. The Carthaginians came originally from Phoenicia, which is approximately present day Lebanon. The Phoenicians, in the ninth century B.C., had established their major colony of Carthage in North Africa (Carthage is now a suburb of the city of Tunis). Being a seafaring people and avid for trade, the Carthaginians began to further explore the shores of the Mediterranean. They established a colony in Sicily at Motya not far from what is today Marsala, which in ancient times was called Lilybaeum. Carthaginian settlements were mostly in the western part of the island, but unlike the Greeks the Carthaginians' interests were purely commercial. Hence, their settlements were not so much colonies as places for anchorage and for trade. They preferred headlands or off-shore islands. For a time they were content with just the single settlement at Motya (modern Mozia) which is a tiny low-lying island. After

Motya, the Carthaginians founded a port at a place known to the Greeks as Panormus (meaning "broad harbor")—now present day Palermo—which they probably called *Ziz* (Phoenician for "flower"). Later they established a site at Solus (Solunto) and a little later at Drepana (Trapani). The latter name is derived the Greek word for "sickle," because of the shape of the peninsula on which the city is located. The nearby Elymian port of Eryx was converted by the Carthaginians into a naval station (that site was revered by ancient sailors as a shrine of the protecting goddess Venus Erycina). But in all, there were not many Carthaginian settlements in Sicily in comparison to the Greek and thus there was, at first, little competition between the two peoples for control of the island. Indeed, it is known that there were Greek settlers and a commercial trade in Greek products at Motya. Conflict between the two peoples only really occurred after the 6th century B.C.

Traditional Greek culture, of course, also had become well-established in Sicily during the periods of colonization. Not only did the Greeks introduce their gods and religion to the island, but many sacred sites of earlier peoples were hellenized or adapted to the Greek cults. Thus, in time, Sicily would be claimed by the Sicilian Greeks to be the place where Demeter, the Greek goddess of the fertility of the earth, first gave grain to man (challenging the traditional site of Eluesis in Greece). And Enna in Sicily was claimed as the site where Hades, the god of the underworld, abducted Demeter's daughter Persephone. According to this popular legend, Hades, the god of the underworld, had deceived Persephone, whom he desired, into paying a visit to the underworld. Once there, she could not return and her mother Demeter, missing her daughter, began to grieve. As she did, all the earth became cold and barren. Crops stopped growing and trees no longer bore fruit. The gods, fearing that this would mean the end of life on earth, had to arrange a compromise. Persephone could spend half the year with her mother. During that time Demeter would be content and the earth would again become warm with all of nature being reborn. But when the daughter had to return to the underworld for the next half of the year, cold and darkness again set in. The cycle of the seasons had been set.

In the same myth-making process, various Sicilian sites were also pointed out by the Greeks as having been visited by other legendary figures, such as the hero Hercules, and the city of Eryx was specifically cited as the home of Aphrodite, the Greek goddess of love and beauty. This last example helped to solidify Greek claims to the northwestern part of the island. Syracuse too, had traditionally been founded at the command of a god, in this case Apollo. And, there was a variation of the legend of the god Dionysos, in Latin called Bacchus, which said that the god first discovered how to produce wine from grapes in Sicily rather than in Greece.

Architecturally, the Greek cities in Sicily resembled those back in Greece and a Greek from Athens or Corinth would have felt quite at home there. In fact, more Greek temples are preserved in Sicily than anywhere else. The Sicilian cities all followed the Hellenic model— each had its central square, or *agora,* surrounded by temples and other public buildings, with the cemeteries being built outside the city itself. From the east, south, and north of the agora streets radiated, each with a colonnade. Then in Greek fashion the western side of the agora was left open.

The oldest of temples in Sicily done in the traditional Greek style called the "doric" is located at Syracuse. It was built around 575 B.C. and was dedicated to the twin deities Apollo and Artemis. It is as old as temples at Olympia back in Greece. Similar buildings were erected at Selinus, Himera, Akragas, and elsewhere, but these later examples have ornamentations which are not found in Greece and therefore can be called distinctly Sicilian, such as the lion rain-spouts at Himera and Akragas. Other slight differences occur because sculptors were guided by the availability of different types of stone on the island. Probably the most impressive of Sicily's classical remains are in the Valley of the Temples at Agrigento where several majestic doric temples are scattered amid groves of olives and almond trees. The sight is especially beautiful at the time of the Almond Blossom Festival that is held there today in February in conjunction with an international folklore festival.

Another important Greek art, the drama, also flourished in Sicily and here too variations appeared such as the introduction of mime to comedy and a different emphasis on the role of the chorus. It was these developments that would later influence the Roman adaptation of the art. It would be wrong, however, to think that the Sicilian Greeks themselves put much emphasis on these differences. They would have preferred to stress, instead, their Hellenic identity and aspects of their cultural unity with the rest of the Greek world. Their emphasis would have been on those factors which served to provide all Greeks with a sense of unity and even superiority to other cultures. Today, in fact, the drama is still presented for a full season at the large and magnificent Greek theater that stands at Syracuse. Modern scholars, using Greek theater masks kept at the Aeolian Museum on Lipari, have been able to accurately reconstruct the ancient models, thus allowing modern actors to portray the roles as they were on the ancient stage. During antiquity it was, of course, relatively easy for the Sicilian Greeks to keep in touch with the rest of the Greek world. There was continuous interchange between Sicily and the homeland and the first colonists continued to attract other settlers. Apart from the commercial traffic there was also constant travel from Sicily back to Greece for various ceremonial and religious functions. Cultural contact was always maintained between the Greek homeland and the western states. The great philosopher and mathematician, Pythagoras, for example, eventually moved to Italy and from there began a stream of philosophic thinking which itself eventually produced formal logic. The study of rhetoric too, became an independent subject in education first at Syracuse and then was brought to Athens by the orator Gorgias. The playwright Aeschylus and the poet Pindar both lived in Syracuse, with Aeschylus spending his last years at Gela. And, the authors Epicharmus and Theocritus were both born in Sicily.

The Sicilian Greeks themselves often returned back to Greece to visit the major shrines, oracles, and festivals and, of course, to participate in the all-important Olympic games. In fact, the records of victors of the games yields the name of the first Sicilian to win in an Olympic event. He was Lygdamis of Syracuse and in 648 B.C. he took the prize for the *pankration*—a combination of wrestling, boxing, and kick-boxing. Legend described him as being as strong as Hercules. Between 572 and 558 B.C. another Sicilian Greek, Tisander of Naxos, took the Olympic prize for boxing four times. Later, the rulers of Sicilian cities, who often won the chariot races at Olympia and at Delphi, would commission victory odes by the famous poet Pindar or set up statues of their victorious chariots. Citizens of the Sicilian cities were also often chosen to represent the Greek mother-city at various other political and religious functions and events.

The Age of the Tyrants

Other developments in the Sicilian cities also paralleled those back in Greece, especially in military and political affairs. First, in terms of the development of military technology, there was the appearance of a new type of soldier—the *hoplite*. This heavily armed infantryman would change the style of ancient warfare, causing chariots for a time to be out of fashion as the use of foot soldiers now dominated ancient battle strategy. However, it was in the area of political developments that the most important changes of the 6th century would occur. Among such changes for Sicily during that difficult period were a growing tension between the Sicilian Greeks and the Carthaginians and, most importantly, the emergence of the tyrants.

The word "tyrant" derives from the Greek term for a single ruler but, as the historical record of these rulers had been so much one of brutality and abuse of power, the word has taken on a negative connotation. The ancient Greek tyrants were unconstitutional monarchs who had exploited the dissatisfaction of the poorer elements of the cities' populations, exhorting them to rise up and follow the new demagogue. The history of Greek Sicily, therefore, becomes the history of those tyrants and clever demagogues who managed to become powerful leaders. They actually outnumbered the tyrants back in Greece and were especially known for their brutality and callous disregard of the rights of their subjects. Yet, the Sicilian tyrants did make contributions, not the least of which was to provide the unity that the island's colonies so badly needed. Often these tyrants employed mercenary troops to enable them to hold on to power or to attack other areas.

One early example was the tyrant Phalaris who, during the years 570 to 555 B.C., became ruler of Aleagris (now Agrigento). His life is somewhat clouded in legend but it is known that he was a member of the wealthy class. It is said that he first seized power by misappropriating a large sum of money entrusted to him for the building of a temple to Zeus. Instead Phalaris used the money to acquire a mercenary force and take control of the city. He ruled for fifteen years, but we know little else about him except that he was accused of committing such monstrous acts as cannibalism—devouring the flesh of infants—and roasting his enemies alive in a huge hollow brazen bull.

Another tyrant was Gelon of Gela who ruled from 485 to 476 B.C. He became so powerful that he was able to take over Syracuse and develop a large army and navy. Gelon used a different technique to maintain power—he transferred half of the population of Gela to Syracuse. In time, he became the most important ruler in the whole of the Greek world.

In the western part of Sicily, another tyrant emerged by the name of Theron. With his forces he was able to attack Himera and between himself and Gelon they ruled most of Sicily. It was at this point that the Cartharginians entered the conflict, having been asked by other Sicilian cities for help. In 480 B.C. the Carthaginians landed in what is now Palermo and proceeded eastward. But they were defeated by

Gelon's forces. Their fleet was destroyed and their soldiers enslaved—the typical fate of those who lost in ancient warfare. Typically, if a tyrant lost he would be remembered most unfavorably, but if he succeeded he often acquired heroic proportions. This is what happened to Gelon. And, in a sense, he did unify large areas of the island and caused enough money to be generated to stimulate its economy.

At this point, the late fifth century, there occurred what might be called a democratic interlude. The ruling class of citizens again exerted their power and tyrants were expelled from most of the Sicilian cities. Democracy, or direct rule by the citizens, was instituted. In the Greek sense, democracy was in fact just that—direct participation by all citizens. Everyone had the opportunity to cast a vote on all the issues put forth by the government and even to serve directly in the government. In this way the citizens of the Greek city or "polis" acted as their own legislature. This was possible, of course, because the number of actual citizens—only free adult males made up that group—was small, usually only a few thousand.

One disadvantage with such a small number of citizens was that a potential tyrant could, through wealth or influence, easily try to take control. To prevent this, the Greeks of the period developed a practice called "ostracism." It was used both in the cities back in Greece and in the colonies, being used, for example, often at Syracuse. In actuality ostracism was simply a call for a vote among the citizens to decide if a particular fellow citizen, who might for some reason become a potential tyrant, should be sent into an honorable and temporary exile. If a majority voted for the exile, he would be sent to live, in moderate comfort and with his expenses paid, outside of the city for a designated period of time. After that he could return. The word ostracism derived from the Greek *ostrakon,* originally meaning a "fragment" then by extension, a "ballot." This comes from the fact that the ancient Greeks used broken fragments of pottery on which they wrote notes or short messages. The fragments also served as ballots during elections. But, the practice of ostracism was easily open to abuse and, in time, it actually caused the better citizens to withdraw from politics altogether. Ostracism was used, in fact, as a weapon by potential tyrants against those who would block their own rise to power.

During this period contact was always maintained between the Sicilian colonies and the mother cities back in Greece or with outside forces. In the late fifth century B.C. the commerical rivalry between Athens and Corinth brought a renewed interest and the signing of several trade treaties between those cities and the colonies. This developed into a conflict reflected in the struggle between the Sicilian cities of Selinus and Segesta. Syracuse was helping Selinus. Segesta asked Athens for help. In 415 B.C. Athens sent a large force and an armada, and in doing so brought Sicily into the long inter-Greek struggle known as the Peloponnesian War.

The Athenian forces consisted of 137 ships, 25,000 sailors, and 7,150 land troops. The invasion, which was led by the general Alcibiades, a follower of Socrates, was a total disaster for the Athenians and a major victory for Syracuse. Alcibiades had been forced to return to Greece before the battle was over and while he was gone his troops became bogged down. Instead of besieging Syracuse they were themselves besieged. In 413 B.C. Athens sent another expedition of 73 ship and 20,000 sailors and infantry but even these could not capture the heavily fortified city. The Athenian forces decided to withdraw but, at that very moment, there was a lunar eclipse which was taken as an omen that the retreat should be delayed. During this time, the Syracusans blocked the Athenian ships in the harbor and the Athenians, unable to escape, lost all that remained of both expeditions. The surviving Athenians were sold into slavery. The failure of this campaign was a great blow to Athens. Syracuse and her allies subsequently joined the Spartan side against the Athenians in the Peloponnesian War. The loss at Syracuse was one of the factors that eventually caused Athens to lose both the war and her place as the leading Greek city-state.

With the Syracusan victory, the city of Selinus was naturally in the ascendency and attacked Segesta anew. This time Segesta asked Carthage for help. In 409 Selinus was captured by the Carthaginians who then marched on to Himera where they defeated the Syracusan forces. Having achieved their purpose the Carthaginians went back home. A Syracusan leader, however, kept attacking Carthaginian centers in Sicily. Then, the Carthaginians came back in earnest. The first attack was on Algergas, which had become a wealthy community. It was an easy victory for the Carthaginian forces, as Syracuse itself was on a downward path. The Carthaginians once again, however, decided to halt. This time an additional development forced that decision—the plague had spread among the Carthaginian forces. The Carthaginians had lost an opportunity to possibly take control of the island.

From this point, 405 B.C., until the Roman conquest which began in 264, the history of Sicily can be described through the reigns of five rulers of Syracuse, with of course, periods of intermittent civil war and internal conflict. The first of these rulers was Dionysius I.

Both Plato and Aristotle considered him a model of duplicity and despotism. Like other despots in history, Dionysius was a leader who emerged during a time of strife and confusion. He achieved power by appealing to the poorer classes, but his aim was personal power. Dionysius first made sure he got the money or at least the equipment and then conscripted labor while employing the use of mercenary forces. He made Syracuse the most fortified and the most populous city in Europe. He also made warfare a science, with a siege-craft being especially developed through the use of trained sappers, mobile towers, and long range catapults. To pay for this Dionysius imposed a twenty per cent tax on the citizens of Syracuse.

His military power increased and in time he controlled most of Sicily with the exception of the northeast region. He was also able to capture the Carthaginian stronghold of Motya. When the plague broke out among the Carthaginian forces Dionysius' military might increased. Prisoners taken were sold as slaves. Then once having achieved power, he began to build public works, to revive trade, to promote literature. Syracuse became the largest Greek city of the period and flourished as the capital of a western Greek empire. For his own safety Dionysius turned the island of Ortygia in the city's harbor into an impregnable stronghold. In fact, there is, just outside the city, an S-shaped cave called the "Ear of Dionysius" that can be visited today. Traditionally, it was where the tyrant could go to overhear the whispered remarks of his enemies who were confined in a nearby quarry. All things considered, Dionysius is probably a good example of dictatorship at its worst. He died in 367 B.C., after a reign of thirty eight years.

After the death of Dionysius I, there was a power struggle in which his brother-in-law Dion emerged for a short time as ruler. Soon, he was exiled by Dionysius II, who was the son of Dionysius I. In 357 B.C., Dion returned and once again there was a contest for control of the island. This lasted until Dion died in 354 B.C. and Dionysius II, who had established a base in southern Sicily, retook Syracuse. The Greek philosopher Plato, who had originally visited Sicily to contact a group of followers of the philosopher Pythagoras and at that time observed first hand the tyranny of Dionysius I, later returned to Syracuse and met Dion. He would subsequently serve as a political advisor to both Dion and Dionysius II. Plato had hoped to educate Dionysius II in the image of his famous "philosopher-king"—the ideal model for a ruler outlined in his most important work, *The Republic*. But in that endeavor, he had little success and abandoned the task.

It was at this point in her history that Syracuse asked for assistance from Corinth back in Greece. It was the first time that a Greek mother-city became directly involved in the domestic affairs of a colony. A commander named Timoleon was sent and, landing at what is now Taormina in 344 B.C. with a small army and few resources, succeeded in taking over most of the area. He, too, was a tyrant. However, once having conquered, he began to make positive contributions, benefiting the city and Sicily in general. Timoleon removed most of the petty tyrants around the island and encouraged the development of the economy. He brought in immigrants and gave them land to farm and succeeded in introducing a modest form of democratic government to the area and especially in Syracuse. For these reasons he is considered among the better rulers of that city-state.

The next tyrant to emerge was Agathocles. He was a different type of ruler, one not ingrained with democratic principles, but rather with military and political ambitions. He would eventually involve Syracuse in a number of imperialistic adventures. First, with the help of veterans and some of the poor, Agathocles was able to engineer a coup d'état. There was bloodshed, with the wealthy classes suffering the most. But finally, promising to uphold the constitution, he became commander-in-chief and from 316 until 304 assumed a political role similar to that of Dionysius I. At this time, Carthage again saw an opportunity to intervene in Sicilian affairs and attacked Syracuse. The two forces fought and at one point in the struggle each army was actually besieging the other's city at the same time. Finally, a peace agreeable to both sides was worked out. Then, in 304 B.C. with all of the island under his control, Agathocles assumed the title of King of Sicily, the first time such a title had been used. He attempted a few more overseas ventures into Italy and the Adriatic, but failed to establish a permanent empire outside of Sicily and died in 289 B.C. At this moment a new people, the Romans, would appear as a rising power in the Mediterranean world and, because of the events just described, they first gained a foothold on Sicily. A new chapter in the island's long history had begun.

III
Roman Province

THE ROMAN PHASE OF SICILIAN HISTORY BEGAN IN THE EARLY THIRD century B.C. Actually, the Roman appearance in Sicily came about indirectly and was the result of the enmity between Rome and her arch-rival Carthage. To understand how this occurred, it is first necessary to examine two earlier developments on the island.

To begin with, there was, during the reign of the tyrant Agathocles, a conflict between the people of Syracuse and a band of hired mercenaries from the Italian mainland called the Mamertines. It had, of course, been a usual practice among the tyrants to make use of mercenaries to help to keep themselves in power. But the Mamertines, whom Agathocles had brought over from Campania and whose name was derived from Mars, the god of war, not only practiced warfare, but banditry and marauding as well. They finally had to be bought out by Agathocles, after which they relocated at Messina. There, they killed or exiled all the men and took the women for themselves, making the city their new base. From Messina they raided as far south as Gela and Kamarina on the coast.

At the same time, there appeared in Sicily a Greek king, Pyrrhus. The ruler of the Balkan kingdom of Epirus, Pyrrhus was a son-in-law of Agathocles and a cousin of Alexander the Great. Like Alexander, he was tempted by visions of world power. Wishing to extend his rule, Pyrrhus took advantage of an appeal from the city of Tarentum (present-day Taranto), on the Italian mainland, to help against the Romans. Tarentum, a Greek colony, wished to assert its independence from the growing Roman power in southern Italy. Traditionally, it is told in Roman history that when a Roman envoy had visited the city to ask for its submission, he was refused a hearing. Instead, the mob he was addressing laughed at his poor Greek and pelted him with filth. To this insult he held up the soiled robe and made the telling reply: "laugh now, but this robe shall remain uncleansed until it is washed in your best blood." Rome was offering peace in exchange for domination. The Tarentines had to prepare for war, and it was then that they asked Pyrrhus for help.

With this invitation from Tarentum, Pyrrhus crossed over into Italy with a large force that included 20,000 infantry, 3,000 cavalry, and 20 elephants. He soon had two victories over the Romans, but his own forces were themselves severely depleted. According to the ancient sources, when he returned to Tarentum to offer the spoils of war in the temple of Zeus, Pyrrhus remarked to a companion who was congratulating him that another such victory would utterly ruin him militarily—hence the term "pyrrhic victory." But soon Pyrrhus saw another opportunity to dominate in Italy and quickly took advantage of a chance to intervene in Sicilian affairs. In 278 B.C. he landed on the island with a force of 10,000 men. In fact, Pyrrhus had been invited by the Sicilian Greeks to help defend them against both the Mamertines and the Carthaginians. He did defeat both groups wherever they were on the island, except for the Carthaginians at their stronghold of Lilybaeum, (present day Marsala), and soon was able to proclaim himself King of Sicily.

At this point one of his lieutenants named Hiero, took over Syracuse and, betraying Pyrrhus, allied himself with the Carthaginians. Hiero assumed the royal title and ruled for 54 years, although his sphere of influence was limited to the southeastern part of the island.

Interestingly, it was for this same Hiero that the famous mathematician Archimedes devised a test to see if one of the king's goldsmiths had been cheating him by making a cup out of a gold and silver alloy. How to find the actual gold content of the cup was, for Archimedes, at first a puzzle until one day upon entering his bath he observed the displacement of the water. Crying "Eureka" ("I have found it"), Archimedes realized that he now had the answer. He had discovered the principle of specific gravity and could apply it to weigh the true gold content of the cup.

Hiero, in order to retain his power and in spite of the fact that he was involved with the Carthaginians, soon allied himself with the Romans. Pyrrhus had already withdrawn ingloriously from the island, harried by the Carthaginian fleet. By now a fierce and bitter rivalry for the control of the Mediterranean had developed between the Carthaginians and the Romans. In this alliance with Hiero the Romans saw the possibility of intervening in Sicilian affairs. Carthage by this time dominated the western Mediterranean. The power of its empire extended from the borders of Cyrenaica in northern

Africa to the legendary pillars of Hercules at the end of the Mediterranean Sea and beyond. Their ancestors, the Phoenicians, had been described by the Greek poet Homer as being "greedy men, famous for their ships," by which he probably meant that they were essentially merchants as well as good sailors. Being a merchant empire, the Carthaginians had a natural interest in maintaining a foothold for trade and shipping in Sicily. But unlike the Romans, they were more content with their possessions and had little liking for war. Instead of raising a citizen army, as the Romans did, the Carthaginians employed mercenaries who were then led by Carthaginian officers.

In 264 B.C., taking advantage of an invitation from the Mamertines of Messina to help them against attacks by both Hiero and the Carthaginians, the Romans invaded the island. Thus, it was the Mamertines who would bring the Romans directly into Sicilian affairs. The Romans, once they intervened of course, came into conflict with the Carthaginians and in that same year the First Punic War would begin. The word "Punic" used to describe the struggle, derives from the Latin word for "Phoenician." Rome was eager to fight but, because Carthage had such a strong navy, the Romans, during this conflict, had to first perfect their own naval techniques and strategies. They developed, for instance, the "corvus" (meaning "crow"), which was a hooked ladder that ran up the side of the mast of a ship and could also drop and latch onto the enemy's vessel, allowing the Romans to board. In fact, the Romans trained their troops to fight in the naval encounters of this war by first practicing with ships beached on land until the soldiers gradually got used to fighting at sea. The Romans wanted to transform naval war into land war and in this effort they were more successful than they had dared hope. Although the war would last a quarter of a century, the Romans succeeded in conquering most of the island. They took Akraga (Agrigento), and twenty-five thousand of its inhabitants were sold into slavery. The same fate awaited Panormus (Palermo). Lilybaeum held out for ten years until 241 B.C. By then all of Sicily would be under Roman control except for the Syracuse area which was held by Hiero, Rome's ally. An interesting monument of this period that can still be seen today in Syracuse is the gigantic Altar of Hiero. It extends for over 200 meters in length and was used for the annual royal sacrifices.

As a result of the Roman conquest, Sicily had to pay an annual tribute, mostly in corn, and the island soon became known as the "granary of Rome." When Hiero died, there were plots and counterplots. He had been succeeded by his inept grandson, Hieronymus, who broke the pact with Rome and formed an alliance with Carthage. Because of this, Rome, in 212 B.C., decided to take over Syracuse and the surrounding region.

Before his death Hiero had entrusted the defenses of the city to Archimedes. Being both scientist and an engineer, Archimedes designed engines and devices that could shoot missiles from the city walls great distances into the Roman fleet. There were even cranes and hooks that could pick up both men and small ships. For several months, the Romans were unsuccessful in their attack on Syracuse. Then the unexpected happened. A mercenary soldier betrayed the Syracusans and opened a strategic city gate to the Romans. The city was conquered and plundered. The Roman commanders sent officers to capture Archimedes as a prize of war, but a common soldier came across him first and cut him down. The last stronghold of Sicily was now in Roman hands.

There would be two more wars between Rome and Carthage. It was during the Second Punic War that Italy was invaded by the famous Carthaginian general, Hannibal. His invasion, in 218 B.C., included the incredible exploit of crossing the Alps into Italy with a large army that included elephants for transport. Hannibal subsequently defeated the Romans at the major battle of Cannae and then announced that in five days his force would reach Rome and he would "dine in the Capitol." Because Rome was so threatened with invasion during this second conflict, the island of Sicily took on additional strategic importance as a barrier between the Carthaginian forces in Italy and their home base in North Africa. From southern Sicily the Romans were able to invade Africa and disrupt communications between Hannibal and Carthage. The second war finally ended in 202 B.C. with a Roman victory over the Carthaginians at Zama in North Africa. There would be peace for a time, but in 149 B.C. the Romans undertook a Third Punic War with the intention of destroying Carthage. That third conflict ended in 146 B.C. with a Roman conquest, and subsequent destruction, of the ancient Phoenician city. For 17 days Carthage burned, then its massive walls were leveled. The Roman commander at the time turned to his lieutenant and said, "I have a foreboding that the same fate may one day befall our own country." But Rome was, at this point, the master of the Mediterranean and the island of Sicily would now be fully incorporated into the empire as a Roman province.

From the time of Roman rule until the year 1860 of our own era, when Sicily would become part of a united Italian kingdom, all independence was suppressed on the island. Roman rule itself over

Sicily lasted six hundred and fifty years. Referring to the island, the great Roman statesman Cicero wrote that it had been the province of Sicily which was "the first to teach our ancestors what a fine thing it is to rule over foreign nations." He also served as an Roman official at Lilibaeum (Marsala) which he called "a most splendid city." In fact, it is the large history of the period written by Cicero that is now one of our main sources of information concerning the events that occurred during this time.

With Sicily, Rome actually gained an "imperial" possession and with it, for the first time, faced the financial problems of empire. To alleviate this burden, the Romans imposed taxes. In the Syracuse region they continued the high annual tribute of ten percent of the harvest that had originally been imposed during the rule of Hiero. Soon they applied the same policy to the rest of the island. Lacking an experienced bureaucracy, the Roman Senate employed private individuals, known as "tax farmers," to collect the revenues. These tax farmers worked by contract and had to take their profits out of what they collected. The position was extremely lucrative and in time the system became quite abusive. The post of tax farmer would actually go to the highest bidder and the tax-payers had to bear the burden. A number of hired guards were available to assist these officials. As a province, Sicily was governed by a prefect or praetor and the island was so rich that this post, too, became a political prize. But the peace that Rome, in turn, brought to the island, did bring benefits and in time Sicily gained a measure of autonomy. It was not, however, to be free from the corruption of government. For a time the province was administered by one of the worst prefects in Roman history, the notorious Verres. Because Rome did not maintain a full standing army in Sicily, Verres was able to easily evade control by the Roman Senate. He misused his position to embezzle funds, confiscate land, art works and property, and to imprison without just cause those who opposed him. Although in the initial period of his administration he may have been a somewhat effective official, he was soon corrupted and with his cohorts embezzled funds and terrorized and looted the population. In three short years he devastated the island and its economy. Only through the efforts of the senator Cicero in 69 B.C. was Verres brought up on charges of malfeasance in office. But he succeeded in avoiding punishment by escaping to Marsiglia (present-day Marseilles).

Cicero, who had been an administrator in Sicily himself, and a few other leading Romans were probably quite familiar with the island. But, in the early years of Roman rule, Sicily was still, in terms of culture and language, mostly Greek. Rome and Italy were, in a sense, foreign nations to the Sicilians. All inhabitants, including the descendants of earlier peoples, now spoke Greek, no matter what their origin had been. Latin was an intrusive and alien language at this time, a fact which the Romans themselves acknowledged. Verres, for instance, had employed interpreters when dealing with the people, and the ancient Sicilian historian Diodorus, who wrote in both Greek and Latin, made it a point to mention that he himself only knew Latin because of his contact with the Romans on the island.

The character of the ancient Sicilians has been described with admiration by Cicero. "A sense of order, frugality, and economy, the love of work, perseverance in their pursuit—qualities that marked the character of our ancestors—are virtues generally found among the Sicilians." In effect, he believed that the Sicilians were the most industrious of all the inhabitants of what had been the ancient Greek world, and acknowledged the predominance of the Greek culture on the island. At this time, contact was still maintained between the Sicilians and the cities of Greece, not only for trade, but for events such as the Olympic games, religious celebrations, and other pan-Hellenic events. Temples and theaters in Sicily were still built in the Greek style, and such typically Roman buildings and structures as the amphitheaters actually did not appear until later. But there were some other very definite changes made in the island's economic and social structure.

It was during the period of Roman rule that *latifundia,* or great agricultural plantations or estates, were established. These estates were operated by means of large numbers of slaves who belonged to wealthy Romans or Sicilians. The Roman author Pliny mentioned one such *latifundium* (literally, "broad farm"), that had a quarter of a million livestock and a population of over 4,000 slaves. Often, the independent peasantry of the island were absorbed as tenants on these huge estates. It was the beginning of an unfortunate system that would in fact prevail until fairly modern times. Conditions on the latifundia were so bad in Roman times that they would cause large slave revolts on the island.

Slavery has always been the curse of mankind, yet even today it still exists in certain forms in various parts of the world. It was particularly bad in the Mediterranean region during the period being discussed. Because of frequent wars or takeovers, thousands of people, white, black, rich and poor, would be enslaved. In Sicily, thousands of slaves were needed to work on the large estates, in quarries, or to serve as herdsmen. The misery of these workers knew no limit.

Prehistoric Village, Panarea, Aeolian Islands. This group of volcanic islands off Sicily's northeast coast was the site of some of the earliest neolithic settlements in the Mediterranean region. The village at Panarea dates from about 4,000 B.C. (Courtesy of the Italian Cultural Institute of New York.)

Temple of Juno, Agrigento. Built in the 5th century B.C., this temple stands in the famous Valley of the Temples, which contains some of the finest examples of Greek architecture. The valley is an especially picturesque site in February, when the temples are framed by the blossoming almond trees nearby. (Courtesy of the New York Public Library Picture Collection.)

Temple of Concord, Agrigento. Considered the most perfect and harmonious example of the Doric style in Sicily or "Magna Grecia," as it was known in ancient times, this 5th century Greek temple was once brilliantly colored in polychrome stucco, as was traditional. (Courtesy of the New York Public Library Picture Collection.)

Greek Theater, Syracuse. Built in the 5th Century B.C., this theater is considered to be one of the finest remaining examples of its kind. It originally held up to 15,000 spectators, and is now used for modern productions of ancient Greek plays. (Courtesy of the Italian Cultural Institute of New York.)

Roman Amphitheater, Syracuse. Built during the Imperial Age, the Roman amphitheater is carved from the surrounding rock and is elliptical in shape. Here, the spectacles of the Roman world were presented, including gladiatorial combats. (Courtesy of the New York Public Library Picture Collection.)

The Roman Villa, Piazza Armerina. First excavated in 1820, a vast Imperial Palace of the 3rd–4th centuries A.D. has as one of its most beautiful features a series of majestic floor mosaics. Depicted is an erotic scene from a bed-chamber. The Villa is considered the most important archaeological Roman find in Sicily.

Domes of the Church of S. Giovanni degli Eremiti, Palermo. The influence of Arabic rule in Sicily is clearly evident in oriental cupolas of the S. Giovanni Church. It was built in 1132, during the reign of Roger II, on the ruins of a mosque which are still visible inside. (Courtesy of the Italian Cultural Institute of New York.)

In ancient times, writers had cautioned the danger of allowing slaves of the same background to work together. If they spoke the same language, it was reasoned, they could easier plan and carry out revolts much more easily. Although the slaves in Sicily did, in fact, come from different backgrounds and cultures, most of them soon came to speak Greek. Thus, when revolts did occur on the island, they were better planned and were on a much larger scale that in the other provinces.

In the year 139 B.C. it was a Syrian slave, Eunus, who organized the first slave revolt in Sicily. A natural leader, Eunus first led the uprising against his wealthy master, a certain Damophilus, who was subsequently killed. The revolt then spread quickly and, gathering support, Eunus soon was able to proclaim himself king of the island with his mistress as queen. Those former slave owners who survived the great uprising were themselves now enslaved and forced to work for their new masters.

At that moment, another revolt took place in the Agrigento region. Here, the leader was a herdsman named Cleon who had agreed to join Eunus. Together they built up a force that eventually numbered 200,000. They rampaged through the area extending from Tauromenium and Morgantina. Only in 132 B.C. was the revolt put down by the Romans who in turn, brutally executed thousands of the slaves turned masters.

Unrest, however, continued and soon a similar revolt occurred in the western part of the island. Here, two leaders emerged. One of them, a slave named Athenion, said it had been foretold in the stars that he would one day be king of Sicily. For this reason, he deliberately did not destroy the crops and livestock of the island as he and his followers rampaged through the region. The earlier slave leader, Eunus, had a similar policy because he, too, had wanted to create a kingdom on the island. Another leader, Salvius, who apparently had had military training, joined Athenion's revolt and, together, they began to push the Roman forces back. But this time, the Romans were better prepared and in 99 B.C. the uprising was totally suppressed. Later, in 70 B.C., there was fear of a slave army invading from the mainland led by the famous gladiator Spartacus. That leader had gathered his forces in southern Italy and was ready to cross over to Sicily, but the plan ended when ships that had been promised him by pirates failed to materialize.

The Sicilian slave revolts were put down with great cruelty, but the fact that they had occurred at least caused the Romans to reconsider their policy towards Sicily. This, in turn, led to some improvements in government. Every year an investigator with high authority was now sent out from Rome. Also, while the main seat of government was still kept at Syracuse, a second center was established at Lilybaeum (Marsala), on the other side of the island. The various cities and towns of Sicily, however, still remained Greek in character, and the Greeks, under Roman supervision, ran practically everything. But, by the end of the first century B.C., this too would begin to change. By that time, Latin was slowly, but inexorably, beginning to infiltrate the administrative, military, and business activities on the island, although the everyday language of the people still remained Greek.

Greater changes for Sicily were still to come, however, with the dramatic events that immediately followed the assassination of the Roman leader, Julius Caesar, in 44 B.C. in Rome. Sicily, because of its strategic location, had always been important to the various military factions that had tried to dominate Roman lands during the early part of the first century B.C. The island had been important even to Caesar as a base for his own rise to power. But, once coming to power, Caesar ruled the Roman world for only a brief period. During that time, however, he made an incalculable and lasting effect upon his nation and upon subsequent history. Thus his untimely death marked the beginning of an important period of transition for Rome and her provinces.

This new era began with a great deal of political strife and upheaval. Two factions emerged immediately in Rome, and each claimed the legacy of power that Caesar had left. One of these factions was made up of those who had fully supported Caesar, during his administration, as absolute ruler. It was led by three individuals, Mark Antony, who was one of Caesar's generals; Octavius, Caesar's young nephew; and Lepidus, a senator. Together, they comprised the new government, known as the Triumvirate, that Caesar in his will had recommended to take his place upon his death. The other faction that contended for power with the Triumvirate was made up of the republicans. It represented those who favored the restoration of the original republican form of Roman government that had been replaced by the dictatorship of Caesar. The main leader of this group was Marcus Brutus who had been one of the conspirators in the assassination plot.

Shortly, war broke out between these two factions and quickly engulfed all of Rome's provinces, including Sicily. For a time, Sicily was held for the republican forces by an able general, Sextus Pompey, who was an enemy of the Triumvirate. His father, Pompey, had been

Caesar's greatest rival. But soon, Sicily was invaded by Octavius who brought the island under the Triumvirate's control in 36 B.C. In the process, the Sicily experienced a devastation that was comparable only to that which had occurred during the Carthaginian wars. Octavius imposed his own rule and taxed the island with a large indemnity.

Soon after this takeover of Sicily, the Triumvirate won the war with the republicans and took control of the rest of the Roman world. But, at that point, a power struggle had also developed within the Triumvirate itself. On one side stood of this conflict stood Octavius, now ruling from Rome. On the other, stood Antony, ruling from his power base in the East. There, he had joined forces with the Egyptian Queen Cleopatra, who was now his wife. Each of these two factions sought to dominate the entire Roman world and, consequently, were soon at war with each other. The outcome of this struggle was finally decided in 31 B.C. at the important naval battle of Actium, fought in the eastern Mediterranean. There, Antony and Cleopatra's forces were totally defeated by the Roman fleet under Octavius. The tragic couple returned to Egypt and committed suicide and Octavius became the sole ruler of Rome. The Roman Senate proclaimed him emperor, granting him the new name of Augustus, "majestic." He quickly set about reorganizing the empire, and Sicily, one of the wealthiest and most important provinces would figure prominently in this new policy of reorganization.

Under Augustus, large amounts of land on the island were declared to be imperial property, while other tracts were given to the veterans of his legions who had helped him come to power. They were encouraged to settle and develop the land. As was the case in other provinces, Roman citizenship was extended to all the island's inhabitants, something that had originally been promised by Julius Caesar. Several Sicilian cities, including Catania, Syracuse, Palermo, and Taomina, were raised to the rank of Roman municipalities, a position that gave them special status under Roman law and made their citizen eligible for administrative careers in the Roman government.

Soon, the Sicilian economy improved and the island again became a "breadbasket" of the empire. An interesting floor mosaic of this period, discovered at Rome, depicts Sicily as one of the four major grain producing provinces. A program of building too, was begun on the island—the ampitheaters of Syracuse and Catania, for instance, were built at this time. We know that the one at Syracuse would later be the site of large gladitorial shows during the reign of the emperor Nero. Aqueducts, theaters, baths, and other amenities of Roman public life also appeared in various Sicilian cities. At Catania today, for example, one can still see the *Odeon,* a small Roman theater for rehearsals and musical competitions. Although the island was considered primarily a grain producing region, the Romans still enjoyed the fine wines that were produced on the island. And even before this time, Julius Caesar, for example, had been known as a connoisseur of Sicilian wines. He was said to especially prefer the sweet Mamertino wine produced in the Messina region.

The period under the Empire was, for Sicily, a time of peace and development. It was the era of the much celebrated *Pax Romana.* No legions were stationed on Sicily and there was not to be a naval force based off the island until the invasion of the Vandals in the fourth century A.D. The province of Sicily became so pacified that, in time, it would be administered simply as a subdivision of the Roman government of Italy. Upper class Romans frequently visited the island during this period, and among early "tourist" attractions mentioned were the sights of Syracuse and excursions to Mt. Etna. The Aeolian islands, too, became a Roman holiday resort during the imperial age, and on the southern coast a spa, located near present day Sciacca, was noted for its hot springs. Emperors too, such as Hadrian and Caligula (who especially preferred Syracuse), also enjoyed visiting Sicily. Some of the largest and most luxurious private residences, or villas, were built at this time—Casale, near Piazza Armerina, being an excellent and well-preserved example. But, while the archeological evidence certainly suggests that the first centuries of imperial Roman rule in Sicily marked a time of prosperity and growth, there was little actually written by the Romans concerning that period itself. Probably one reason for this was the fact that the island was relatively peaceful and free from strife and conflict. As such, it gave the Roman administrators there few worries and, consequently, gave the government back in Rome little cause for concern.

There were, of course, other historic developments, and it was during the early years of the Roman Empire that Christianity first appeared in Sicily. Most likely, the earliest Christians there were found among the Jewish communities that existed in the eastern part of the island (St. Paul stopped and preached at Syracuse on his way to Rome) but, in time, the new religion reached the other areas. As was the case elsewhere in the Roman Empire, Sicily was also the home to several other ancient religions and cults. Temples could be found dedicated to the Egyptian goddess Isis or to middle-eastern gods, as well as the traditional Greek and Roman deities. The Persian god Mithras was especially popular among the Roman legionaries. But in time, Christianity, became the most successful of the new faiths.

In 313 A.D., when the emperor Constantine issued the Edict of Milan that lifted the ban on Christianity, the religion spread throughout the island, although its growth was slower in the countryside than in the cities. One interesting development followed. As Christianity emerged in Sicily, churches were, of course, built and dedicated to the early saints of the various regions, including St. Lucia and St. Marcianus at Syracuse and St. Agatha at Catania. But the catacombs, the burial places of the early Christians, that also served as secret meeting places when the religion was forbidden, still continued to be built in Sicily while elsewhere in the empire the practice had been abandoned. An outstanding example of this is the S. Giovanni Catacomb in Syracuse that can be visited today.

With the official recognition and acceptance of Christianity by the Roman government (by the end of the fourth century A.D., it had become the state religion), a new period of history can be said to have begun. For Sicily, this meant entering the orbit of a new and rising power, the Byzantine or Eastern, Empire. From its center at Constantinople, the Byzantine Empire, the successor to the Roman, reached west across the Mediterranean and in a short time, brought the island of Sicily under its control. Sicilian history would enter a new and dynamic period.

IV
The Byzantines

BY THE LATE THIRD CENTURY A.D. THE ROMAN EMPIRE HAD REACHED its geographic limits, extending from Britain to North Africa and from Spain to the Middle East. Because of its size, the emperors of the period, finding it difficult to rule and administer this vast territory from one capital, decided to divide the Empire into two parts, the western and the eastern. The line of demarcation between these areas ran through the Adriatic Sea and the center of the Mediterranean to North Africa. Each half of the empire would have its own ruler, actually a co-emperor, and its own capital. The capital of the West was to remain at Rome, while in East, the emperor Constantine, in the fourth century, chose the city of Byzantium on the Bosphorus as the new center for the Eastern empire. The city was given the name of Constantinople. In time it was to become the center of a new culture as well—the Byzantine.

In 313 AD. Constantine, in his famous Edict of Milan, legalized Christianity. From that time on, the religion spread extensively throughout Roman territory. As a distinct Byzantine culture slowly emerged, so did the eastern form of Christianity, also known as the Byzantine. The Eastern Church, with it center at Constantinople, would be Greek in its style, ritual, and tradition; the Western became Latin with its authority centered in the Pope at Rome. In time, a rivalry developed between the two Churches. Although Sicily would be, in terms of official ecclesiastical jurisdiction, under the Roman Church or the Pope, politically, and in terms of its actual religious orientation, the island would be within the Byzantine sphere of influence.

By the fifth century, the Western Roman Empire was beginning to lose it disciplined military stance as barbarian tribes began to attack its borders. A series of tribal invasions ensued which also engulfed Sicily. Beginning in 429 A.D. such a force, the Vandals, launched a series of invasions from North Africa. Finally, in 468, under their chieftain Gaiseric, they took military control of Sicily. Then, after a brief time, the island came under the control another German chieftain, Odoacer, who would soon proclaim himself King of Italy. It was during this period, because of other barbarian invasions from the north, that Italy again became almost totally dependent on Sicilian grain as other sources had now been shut off. Sicily, of course, was herself never completely free from disturbance and, on one occasion, the island only escaped a particularly fierce barbarian attack, that of the Visigoths under Alaric, because of a storm in the Straits of Messina that blocked the invading forces.

By the end of the fifth century, Sicily and the rest of Italy had become an area of contention between the Goths, one of the largest of the Germanic tribes, and the Byzantines. Finally in 533, one of the most powerful rulers of the Byzantine Empire, the Emperor Justinian, sent his general Belisarius to expel the Vandals from Sicily and restore order. Belisarius, as described by the ancient chroniclers, must have seemed the ideal commander. Tall and handsome, he arrived in Italy already with a great reputation, being known for his humility and generosity as well as for his military prowess. It was said that horses and weapons lost by his men in battle were replaced by the general at his own expense, a most unusual policy at that time. A just administrator, he never permitted his men to loot grain or food in occupied territories.

His landing in Sicily was relatively easy, and he was able to subdue Syracuse and Catania without interference. Only in Palermo did the Goths offer resistance. This, Belisarius quickly and ingeniously quelled by sending his fleet into the harbor with the smaller boats filled with archers who had been lifted up to the mastheads. From there, towering above the city's walls, these archers were able to fire their arrows into the city and force the Goths into submission. Belisarius then returned to Syracuse and celebrated a triumph by scattering gold coins through the crowd that had assembled to greet him. In this way, Sicily was rather quickly brought into the Byzantine orbit. The population itself did not resist, probably because it was Greek and also because the people may have believed Byzantine rule would bring order. The Byzantine administrative system was introduced, and in the Pragmatic Sanction of 554, a proclamation issued by the Emperor Justinian, property that had been taken by the Ostragoths from the landed aristocracy and the Church was restored. Also, a number of other measures to relieve the rest of the population that had been ruined by years of warfare were outlined. (On a negative note, it was during this period that the anopheles mosquito first appeared on the island bringing with it the curse of malaria). As a result of this conquest, which included Dalmatia and Italy, as well as Sicily, Justinian's empire was doubled.

In terms of religious jurisdiction, however, Sicily was still officially under the authority of the Roman papacy which itself maintained large holdings on the island. But the majority of the population followed the rites and practices of the Greek or Eastern Church and, it was at this point, the late sixth century, that various religious disputes began among the Christians of the Byzantine empire. These doctrinal disputes soon developed into the conflicts that, in time, spread to all portions of the empire. Some of these disputes had originated as dogmatic debates over the nature of Christ or similar theological issues. In an age when religious questions were paramount, these controversies grew into struggles that would severely divide the Eastern Empire itself into rival religious factions. Out of such conflicts, diverse Eastern churches appeared, such as the Egyptian and Syrian, which had broken with the Eastern Orthodox Patriarch of Constantinople. Later, other churches that recognized the authority of that Patriarch while developing along national lines, such as the Bulgarian and Russian Orthodox churches, would emerge.

It was because of these controversies as well as other internal conflicts, mostly centered in the eastern regions of the Byzantine empire, that the Emperor Constans II in 663 made the decision to move his capital from Constantinople to a more westerly location. Leaving Constantinople, Constans started out for Italy by way of Athens, and after a sojourn in Rome, Naples, and the south of Italy, decided to establish his court at Syracuse. In choosing that city he may have been following a plan first conceived by the Emperor Justinian to rule the empire from a more centralized location. The result was that Syracuse would become the capital of the Byzantine Empire for five years. But during that time it became apparent that the cost of supporting such an administration was extremely expensive for Sicily to bear. Also, there was dissatisfaction with Constans's tyrannical rule and his failure to bring order to the empire. None of his original projects had been accomplished, his struggle against the Lombards in the north remained unsuccessful, and Sicily was still constantly menaced by the Arabs. Finally, in 668, Constans was assassinated while in his bath by a courtier who struck him fatally on the head with a soap-dish. Upon this emperor's death, the government returned to Constantinople.

The next Byzantine emperor, Heraclius, now ruling from Constantinople, sought to solve some of the problems of the empire by reorganizing various parts of it into "themes," or military provinces. Because of maritime attacks from the Arabs in North Africa, Sicily, like other areas of the empire, was on the defensive. It therefore became one of the first provinces to be designated a theme. As such, the island was governed by a *stratagoi* or military commander. In these new military districts, however, the civil authorities did not immediately give way to the military rulers. In most cases, the civil administration continued to coexist with the new military order. But the military authorities were invested with supreme powers in matters related to any external security and, because of this, tended to more and more make themselves felt more strongly in the civil administration.

During the eighth century, as the Byzantines continued to rule in Sicily, the island became involved in a another great internal religious struggle of the Eastern Empire—the Iconoclastic Controversy. Again, a religious question would become an issue of major importance in the in the political life of the Byzantine Empire. This time, the controversy centered on the debate over the traditional use of icons, or holy images, in the Byzantine churches. The practice of venerating icons was very old and those who supported it believed that it was justified in Christian tradition and teachings. Those who opposed such a usage—the iconoclasts—believed the practice to be pagan and idolatrous. This great controversy spread to all parts of the empire, reaching also Sicily.

There, the population generally supported those who upheld the use of the icons. Because of this, many refugees from the east would come to the island to escape the persecutions led by those emperors who opposed the veneration of the icons. In fact, it was such an iconoclastic emperor, Leo III, who, in order to regulate and increase the financial income of the empire needed for many of his projects, raised the poll tax in Sicily and Calabria by one third. To carry out this measure effectively Leo ordered that records be kept of the birth of all male children. Chroniclers of the time, hostile already to his iconoclasm, compared this order to the actions of the ancient pharoah of Egypt at the time of the Biblical Exodus.

The iconoclastic struggle sharply divided the Eastern Empire for several decades. It was only finally resolved in 843 with the Restoration of Orthodoxy issued during the reign of the Empress Irene. In that imperial edict, the icons were ordered restored to the Eastern Churches, and again became an integral part of the Byzantine liturgy and the private devotions of the people.

It was during the period of Byzantine rule that Sicily, because its

Greek population was steadily increasing, once again became heavily hellenized. In the sixth and seventh centuries many Greeks were forced to leave their country for southern Italy and Sicily under the pressure of Slavonic invasions into Greece. In the seventh century a huge Greek emigration to Sicily took place among populations fleeing Byzantine areas taken by the Persians and Arabs. And in the eighth century, a large number of Greek monks and clergy came to the island fleeing persecution by the iconoclastic emperors. Near Palermo today, in a beautiful country region, can be seen the town of Piana degli Albanese, until this century known as *Piana dei Greci,* a community originally settled during the Byzantine period and where the people still preserve their distinctive dialect and follow the rites of the Eastern Church.

But, it was also at the time of the Byzantine development that Sicily also became the goal of conquest for a new and rising power of the Mediterranean world, the Arabs. Finally, by the tenth century, the island would be taken by this new force and another era in its political and cultural history would begin.

V
The Arabs

WITH THE ADVENT OF ISLAM IN THE SEVENTH CENTURY A.D., ARAB forces, first under the leadership of the Prophet Mohammed, swept north out of Arabia and across the Mediterranean region conquering all who stood in their path. By 650 A.D. the Arabs, or Saracens as they were also known, had taken most of North Africa and were beginning to invade various areas in Europe, including Sicily. Although the spread of Islam was gradual, in time, Moslem armies would take Spain, invade France, and even besiege Rome. It was obvious that Sicily would soon become a target. At first, the island was subject only to periodic raids. But even as early as the mid-seventh century, in the time of the Byzantine emperor Constans II, Arab ships of the Caliph Muawiya had begun attacks on several Byzantine provinces, including Sicily. Often, however, the Arabs were defeated at sea by the Byzantines and, for the time being, the island was safe.

Then, in the ninth century, a full scale Arab invasion of Sicily was begun in earnest. The earlier raids had only really been for pillaging, and to take slaves and supplies. In this later effort, there was a real desire to take control and colonize the island. The invading forces were now large and well organized and included Berbers, Spanish Moslems, and Sudanese from Africa, as well as the Arabs themselves.

The Arabs' objective of a total conquest of Sicily was facilitated when, in 827, a Byzantine administrator on the island named Euphemius organized an uprising against the emperor Michael II and proclaimed himself ruler of the Eastern Empire. But soon, Euphemius realized that his own army would never be strong enough to resist the imperial forces that would be sent by Constantinople. He therefore appealed to the Arabs for help. The Arab forces arrived in Sicily, but instead of helping Euphemius, themselves began a conquest of the island. Euphemius was eventually killed by supporters of the Byzantine emperor as the Arab takeover continued. Half of Sicily was overrun by 860 (Palermo and its surrounding region having been taken some thirty years earlier). At that point, only really Syracuse, of all the large Sicilian cities, remained in the hands of the Christians. Because the Arabs were nearer to their home base in Tunisia, only a day's voyage away, they had the advantage of a constant availability of supplies and reinforcements. Their armies were formidable and their navy probably made use of the famous "Greek Fire"—a substance made from the sulphur and naptha available on the island and shot from flame throwing devices. Greek Fire, which was originally invented by a Sicilian Greek, had once been used successfully by the Byzantines during their wars of conquest.

With the fall of Syracuse in 878, Sicily was now for all purposes under Arab domination. There were some areas of resistance. Taormina, for instance, which was the last important fortified point of the Byzantines, held out until 902. But, by 965, the rest of the island would be taken and would pass totally under Arab control. With the conquest of Syracuse, which had been the political center of the island for fifteen hundred years, the center of power was now transferred to Palermo. Syracuse, once the rival to ancient Rome, Athens, and Alexandria, was devastated and from that time on, Palermo was to be the major city and seat of administration on the island. After becoming the capital of the Arab Emirate of Sicily, Palermo became a center of a cultural assimilation that was developed during the Arab conquest of the Mediterranean region and the Middle East. The city even helped to contribute a "pseudosaint," Aristotle, to the Islamic calendar. The Arabs, taking over much that was Greek on the island, soon found Greek science and metaphysics compatible with their own intellectual bent, and for instance, venerated Aristotle as the most renowned of ancient scholars. It was through Arab commentaries and translations that the Western world first rediscovered several of Aristotle's works, and Sicily, especially Palermo, by virtue of its intellectual associations, became a focus for such activity—a clearinghouse for Aristotelian scholarship. During this time literacy, in general, rose on the island.

But the Arab conquest, of course, also marked the end of official Byzantine and Christian rule. For the next two centuries, the Moslem religion and culture would dominate. In their administration of Sicily, the Arab, or Saracen, rulers followed the Islamic policy of toleration towards Christians and Jews. In practice, this meant that these groups had to pay heavier taxes, wear distinctive clothing, and defer to the Moslems, but otherwise they could practice their respective religions and remain basically unmolested. Of course, many of the island's churches were converted into mosques. All this was standard practice throughout the Islamic world. But besides this, the Christians and Jews were, in general, left alone and were even permitted to retain a measure of self government within their local communities. Actually, as in Spain, Moslems remained a minority ruling a Christian majority and, also as in Spain, relations between the rulers and their subjects varied in the districts into which the country was divided. That difference is, in a sense, still meaningful today. Western Sicily was the Val di Marzala where Moslems were the most numerous and where the majority of Christians were farmers; southeastern Sicily was the Val di Noto where Moslems were few and Christians enjoyed considerable autonomy; northeastern Sicily was the Val di Demone where Christian communities paid tribute to Moslem overlords, but were otherwise free.

In certain other ways too, this new regime was actually less repressive than the old. In terms of economic policy, for example, the Arabs seem to have been more enlightened than the earlier Byzantines, imposing lower taxes with incentives given to encourage agricultural productivity. As Islam was generally more sympathetic than Christianity to the plight of agricultural slaves, it fostered the growth of a free class of peasants who would have an interest in increasing production. And, being part of the Arab empire, Sicily also now had a share in the extensive trading network of the Moslem world that extended from Africa and Europe to Asia.

Palermo, during this period, grew as a center, and various contemporary accounts describe the inhabitants as being not only Arabs and Greeks but Lombards, Persians, Jews, Africans, and Tartars. The city probably had a population of at least 100,000, making it second only in size to Constantinople in both the Mediterranean and European world. Catania, too, developed and was noted for its dozens of mosques.

Arab culture soon spread throughout Sicily and, along with contributions to the sciences and the arts, architecture, and mathematics, there were also considerable developments in agriculture. These developments helped to increase the productivity and output of the island. Rivers were made navigatable, irrigation was improved, and the use of hydraulics was greatly increased. Sugar cane, cotton, mulberries, citrus fruits, date palms, melons, pistachios and other agricultural products were now introduced. The area surrounding Palermo, an artificially irrigated and fertile fruit growing plain, is in fact, known today as the *Conca d'oro,* the "Golden Shell" a beautiful and lush valley, with a wide arc of imposing mountains forming the background.

Under Arab rule, the island's metal mining was also expanded and from the mines silver, mercury, lead, and other minerals were extracted. The production of sea salt, too, became a large industry, and the art of silk weaving and manufacturing also begin to play an important role in the economy. More settlers came from North Africa and there was a corresponding increase in small landholdings. It must be noted however, that due to the need for timber in North Africa, there was extensive deforestation during this period from which Sicily would not effectively recover. Also, due to the repeated invasions by different peoples since the fifth century, there had been extensive damage to the olive groves. Thus, olive production, once an important part of the economy, by the Arab period, had dropped. Olive growing and olive oil production on Sicily would not increase again until later times.

After the Moslem invasion, Arabic of course, became the language of administration, and Arab place names, such as Gibel and Calta, began to appear on the island. The town of Enna was renamed Kasryanni (eventually to become Castrogiovanni), Agrigento became Kirkent, and Lilibaeum was changed to Marsala, the "port of Allah." Many Arabic terms and phrases also entered the language, and in fact, it was only became of the later Norman invasion of the island in 1060 that the Sicilian language did not develop into one resembling those of Malta and North African regions.

In fact, Arab control of Sicily was destined to be short-lived. By the 11th century there began a certain decline of power in the Arab world. Dynastic struggles among the Arabs, beginning since the tenth century had weakened central authority on Sicily itself. Various Arab families, specifically the Aghlabids, the Kalbids, and the Zirids, fought for control of the island and it was the Kalbid emir who finally made a treaty with the Byzantines in order to gain support for his claims to Sicily. In 1030, a Byzantine force led by the general George Maniaces took advantage of this and landed near Messina. Mercenaries in this army included the Russian soldiers of the Varangian guard and several hundred Norman and Scandinavian adventurers including Harald Hardrada, the hero of Nordic saga who later invaded England. Maniaces occupied much of the eastern part of the island for several years, his armies causing extensive damage in the area. It was at that time that the Normans first had the opportunity to observe the wealth of the island and consequently planned their own later raids. This last serious Byzantine attempt to retake the island failed when Maniaces was recalled because of political intrigues back in Constantinople.

However, there were now also conflicts growing throughout the extensive Arab empire, and the power disputes among the Arab dynasties on Sicily still continued. The moment was right for another force to come and attempt to conquer the island. This time it would be the Normans who, in the mid-eleventh century, launched their invasion and began the next phase in Sicily's history.

Although relatively brief, the period of Arab rule in Sicily left its mark. The introduction of a new culture, with its scientific learning and approach to the arts, the improvement of agricultural techniques and the introduction of new and productive crops, all contributed to the making of a vital Sicilian economy and culture. These all would be added factors contributing to the rich and diverse heritage of the island.

VI
The Normans

During the eleventh century adventurers from French Normandy first appeared in southern Italy. These adventurers hired themselves out as mercenary fighters, with some of them supplementing their activities by engaging in pillaging, robbing, and cattle raiding. The Byzantines themselves had hired such mercenaries but some of these, in turn, encouraged by the Papacy, attacked the Greek Christians.

Among the Norman mercenaries in Italy were the several sons of a Norman nobleman, Tancred de Hauteville. Two of his sons, Robert and Roger, together came to control a large area of Apulia and Calabria. Robert had even been strong enough to take the Pope, Leo IX, hostage in 1056. Then, with the approval of later popes, the brothers extended their claims in southern Italy. Norman mercenaries had already freed the city of Salerno from paying tribute to the Arabs and they soon hoped to extend their own influence to Sicily. Having served there as mercenaries for the Byzantines, they were aware of the potential wealth and power to be gained if the island were taken.

In Sicily, factions among the Arabs were fighting amongst themselves and trying to establish separate power bases at Mazara, Girgenti, and Syracuse. In 1061 the Emir, or Arab ruler, of Girgenti asked the Normans for help. Roger de Hauteville crossed the straits of Messina with sixty knights, scouted the area and, returning shortly with a larger force, captured the city of Messina. This occurred in 1061, five years before the Norman conquest of England. In a brief time, Roger controlled all of the northeast region of the island. A first attempt to take Palermo failed but, in time, the Normans, slowly but steadily, conquered the rest of Sicily. Although the Papacy did not provide money or arms to help in what was in effect, the first crusade against Islam, the Pope did give his approval to Norman rule on the island. By 1071, Norman forces finally took Palermo and established their own administration. Actually, Moslem soldiers who had converted to Christianity formed an important part of this army of conquest. The Normans were now strong enough to make treaties with Arab emirates in North Africa, and Sicilian grain was again exported to that region. The final and most destructive stage of the Norman conquest of Sicily then commenced and by 1091, the last Moslem stronghold at Noto fell. The Byzantines at this time had themselves planned to recapture Sicily, but the presence of the Norman forces prevented such an action.

The Norman conquest of the island brought with it certain basic and rather important changes. Latin Christianity slowly began to replace the Greek Church, although the latter continued to prosper for some time after the invasion. The Latin language, too, began to displace Greek as the language of administration and learning, but this also was a slow process. In fact, the Norman settlers on Sicily actually had an impact quite disproportionate to their numbers. In the case of this invasion, there was never a massive immigration as there has been with the Greeks and Arabs. Yet important transitions occurred because of the Normans' keen political ability to adapt to new circumstances. Realizing that they had conquered a superior culture with an efficient administrative system already in place, the Normans co-opted both, and then set about improving the overall structure. In religious and cultural matters, Roger de Hauteville, or Altavilla, as the dynasty came to be known in Italian, followed a policy of toleration towards the many diverse peoples and religions of the island—the Latins, Greeks, Jews, and Arabs, for instance, would each be judged and governed by their own laws and traditions. And, although other members of the Hauteville family had joined the First Crusade, which had been called by the Pope against the Moslems in the East, Roger refused to take part and did not even order all of the Arab troops that had joined his forces after the conquest to convert to Christianity. Through a skillful use of the various cultures and traditions of the island Roger, who had begun as a landless adventurer, became one of the most successful rulers of the age, bringing to Sicily the beginnings of a golden century—unrivaled in terms of prosperity and power by anything since the time of the ancient Greeks.

One specific method of concentrating power that was employed by Roger was his successful combination of the Norman tradition of feudal loyalty to the ruler that he had brought from the north, with the structure and efficiency of the administration that had been left by the Byzantines. But, while fostering the Greek culture and supporting the Greek monasteries on the island, he also initiated a definite policy of Latinization. At the same time, of course, Roger was careful not to antagonize the Moslem population that remained. Lofty Arab titles and customs, in fact, were kept by the new rulers to reinforce their status among the people.

While allowing the growth of Latin Christianity, Roger kept the Byzantine tradition of state control of the Church. This policy had always given the Eastern Emperors power in matters of ecclesiastical governance. For example, Roger gradually introduced French Catholic clerics to administer the dioceses of the island but did not restore the large patrimony of the Roman Church that had been confiscated by the Byzantines. And, although the Pope, Urban II, eventually came to visit the island, Roger still imposed his own will and forced the Papacy to concede to him and his Norman heirs, the title and powers of an Apostolic Legate. With that title, he would have a status and authority approaching that of the Byzantine Emperors in issues regarding church authority. This union of civil and ecclesiastical roles made Roger one of the most powerful rulers of the day. In time, it would become an important point of controversy between the rulers of the island and the Church. Roger also reserved for himself and his family large areas of conquered territory in both Sicily and Calabria. His power increased greatly and, before he died in 1101, he was able to arrange marriages for two of his daughters to both the King of Hungary and the Western Emperor and leave to his son, Roger II, a unified and prosperous kingdom.

Roger I's son and successor, Roger II, ruled not only Sicily and Calabria but also Apulia which he conquered in 1127. He proclaimed all of southern Italy to be part of a new kingdom, the "Kingdom of Sicily," reserving for himself the title "Rex Siciliae et Italiae." He was to become one of the most remarkable rulers of the Middle Ages. Roger II's upbringing reflected the cosmopolitan nature of his Sicilian homeland. He was educated in both Greek and Arabic, as well as French and Latin, and maintained a court reminiscent of those of Byzantine and Moslem rulers. The royal palace at Palermo, for instance, was equipped with all the luxuries and splendors of the eastern capitals. And, his chief advisors continued to use the grand title reminiscent of the Arabic and Greek empires. The chief minister, for example, held the lofty title of "Emir of Emirs and Archonte of Archontes." Significantly, Roger II used his own coronation ceremony to underscore his unique and lofty status, deliberately incorporating into it aspects of the Byzantine and eastern coronation rituals. This was done because he wanted to emphasize that he was more than a king in the western sense. Instead, he wished to be recognized as a ruler in the Byzantine sense, one who received his authority, according to belief, not from the pope or the Western Emperor, but from Heaven alone. A mosaic in the cathedral of Palermo depicts just such a concept, with Roger dressed in both in the insignia of a Byzantine emperor and an Apostolic Legate and symbolically receiving his crown from Christ Himself.

In administrative matters, Roger II followed his father's policy of employing different legal systems to govern the various peoples of the island while, at the same time, encouraging the development of an overall system that would reflect the traditions of Roman, or western, legislation. Roger himself maintained the special position as the direct feudal overlord of the Norman and Lombard landowners. In religious matters, he used the Apostolic Legateship to claim wide jurisdiction and control what was, in effect, a type of national church. In all areas of society, he encouraged building and growth and made many endowments to the monasteries—the traditional centers of learning of the period. Under his rule, Sicily became a major European power and the seat of a Mediterranean empire.

Like his father, Roger II did not have an interest in the religious goals of the crusades, but instead would use them as excuses to extend his own power in the eastern Mediterranean. During the Second Crusade, his armies overran Greece and plundered its larger cities. One result of this was that many expert silk weavers were taken from Greece by the Normans back to Sicily where they would foster the further development of that industry on the island. After this campaign, North Africa, an important strategic base and potential economic market, occupied the plans of King Roger. In 1150, having taken advantage of dispute among the North African rulers, Roger had his forces successfully occupy that region. Settlers were brought in and for a time Roger even styled himself "King of Africa."

In Sicily itself Roger II encouraged the development of agriculture and of several diverse industries, including the production of luxury items, mining, and fishing. He may have had the largest revenue of any king in Europe and his income from Palermo alone itself probably exceeded all the revenues collected by the Norman rulers of England during the same period. Lying midpoint in the Mediterranean and with several excellent ports, Sicily flourished, as the trading network that had developed, grew. And, the island still continued to be the home to varied and diverse cultures. There were now close ties between Sicily and Norman England; Odo of Bayeux, William the Conqueror's brother was buried in Palermo cathedral, and several other English clerics, including Walter of the Mill, or "Offamilo" as he was known in Sicily, served as archbishops of that city.

Immigration from the north increased. There were large Lombard settlements, for example, and the culture of France and the French court began to appear and spread throughout the island. The famous Sicilian marionette shows, still to be seen today, were derived from the French and Provençal jongleurs and bards who brought the legend of Charlemagne to Sicily during this period. The blending of cultures, now typical of the island, continued and, as an example of this, the Byzantine-style court robes of the ruling Normans could be seen decorated with embroidered passages from the Bible written in Arabic letters. Roger's court at Palermo, in particular, was a center of the arts and sciences. There, the study of astronomy was encouraged and scholarly translations were made into Latin of Plato, Euclid, and Ptolemy. The continuation of the Sicilian-Arabic literary tradition was also encouraged. But perhaps nowhere else is the fact that Sicily, during this period, was the meeting place of so many cultures more clearly represented than in the remaining architecture and decorative arts of the age.

Latin basilicas built at this time, for instance, are crowned with Greek cupolas and decorated inside with mosaics done by Arab workmen who employed themes derived from Middle Eastern and Persian mythology. Because so many Byzantine churches in the Eastern Empire were destroyed during the later Turkish invasions, those examples still surviving in Sicily are considered among the best. The church of St. John of the Hermits, built by Roger II, with its fine red domes, seems as much a mosque as a church, and the cathedral at Monreale, built for a Latin bishop, is done in the Romanesque style but inside is decorated with Byzantine mosaics, including the most famous "Christ Pantokrator." Then, there is the great cathedral of Cefalù. This cathedral actually had an interesting beginning. King Roger was sailing back to Sicily from Italy when his ship encountered a terrible storm. Convinced that he was in danger of shipwreck and drowning, Roger swore to build a cathedral wherever he safely came ashore. He landed at Cefalù and that is where the cathedral was built.

Perhaps the finest example of the architecture of the period is Roger's palace chapel at Palermo. Built in the first half of the twelfth century, it incorporates Arabic, Byzantine, and Western motifs and designs. Although much of the palace has been altered, the royal chapel and Roger's private rooms survive in all their original splendor. The chapel, with its brilliant Byzantine mosaics, is a blaze of glory, and the Islamic element of Roger's court is strikingly present in the fantastic wooden stalactites of the ceiling. Although Roger's private room is hard to find, it is well worth seeking out. Its mosaics are as splendid as those of the chapel and are done with equally lavish gold backgrounds. But here, the subjects are secular, with palm trees and such creatures as lions, leopards, deer, swans, and peacocks. It is unlike any other palace of the time.

Roger II was succeeded in 1154 by his son William I. His reign began at a difficult time. There was now growing opposition to the monarchy from the feudal nobility and an increase in racial tensions on the island. Also, in William's first years as king, there were serious military defeats, especially in North Africa, where important bases were lost. The Papacy too, at this time, declared that the powers of the Apostolic Legateship were to be limited just to Sicily alone. William's reign also was marked by struggles and warfare among his feudal barons, and his ministers, too, were generally unpopular. When he died in 1166, he was given the surname of "the Bad." But his son William II, who succeeded him, would instead be called "the Good." This is because, although William II's policies really differed very little from his father's, the twenty years of his reign were more tranquil. One reason for this is that the infighting among the nobility had, for a time, ceased. William II actually lived very much like an oriental potentate, with Arab bodyguards, concubines, and a court that kept the style and traditions of the East. While the Latin Christianizing of the island continued, William II was himself probably indifferent to religion and tolerant of the other faiths in Palermo. He did, however, continue the policy of his Norman predecessors of endowing the large Catholic monasteries. During his reign, the great abbey at Monreale, already mentioned, was built, combining the mixture of styles now common in Sicilian architecture. Located a few miles from Palermo, the Monreale cathedral is considered the finest example of Norman architecture in Sicily. It incorporates Byzantine and Islamic features, such as brilliant mosaics and decorated archways, as well as the forms of Italian Romanesque. The roof can be reached by stairway and offers a spectacular view of the surrounding countryside.

William II, like his predecessors, had ambitions to extend his power overseas, especially in East, where he hoped to become emperor, but he died in 1189 before those plans could be realized.

Taken together, the reigns of Roger II, William I, and William II are generally regarded as comprising a golden age in Sicilian history. For almost a century the island was the center of a powerful, creative, and prosperous kingdom. Palermo became a leading capital of Europe and the Norman Hauteville dynasty succeeded in unifying the various cultures of Sicily, bringing a sense of harmony to these very diverse elements. Politically, while the pope remained the official overlord of the kingdom, the Hautevilles had won, from the Papacy, the title and privileges of the Apostolic Legateship. The acquisition of this important ecclesiastical title would greatly enhance the royal power, especially in the earlier years of the dynasty. Although there were plots and rebellions later on, and more in the reign of William I, these were limited to the Norman feudal aristocracy. The people themselves were satisfied with an administration that seemed to bring more justice and prosperity than had been known for generations. And, there was, of course, a flourishing of the arts. But, with the death of William II at the young age of thirty-six, a rivalry soon began for the succession that would affect the very peace of the kingdom.

William II's heir was his father's half sister, Constance, a daughter of Roger II. She was married to Henry of Hohenstaufen, who was the eldest son of the German Emperor, Frederick Barbarossa. On William's death, Henry and Constance claimed their inheritance which had been ratified by a parliament at the time of their betrothal. But, in both Sicily and on the mainland, there was opposition among all classes to a German king. The barons of the kingdom supported instead Tancred, Count of Lecce, an illegitimate grandson of Roger II. The general population also preferred a Norman ruler. At first Henry was too preoccupied acting as regent in Germany for his father, who had left on the Third Crusade, to travel south and claim the Sicilian inheritance. Tancred meanwhile, had taken the title, but his brief reign was not peaceful and when he died in 1194, Henry, who with his own father's death, had become emperor, proceeded south to take the throne of Sicily. He was crowned at Palermo on Christmas Day in that same year. A new dynasty, the German Hohenstaufens, now ruled the island and a new phase in Sicilian history would begin.

VII
The Hohenstaufens

THE NORMAN KING TANCRED'S BRIEF REIGN IN SICILY HAD BEEN AN uneasy period marked by many problems, including racial unrest. Once again, risings against the Moslem population of the island took place, this time causing a large emigration of a most productive element of the population. The Arabs, unlike the Greeks, had never been completely assimilated and other Sicilians were jealous of their territorial possessions and their positions in the state bureaucracy. This civil war, which broke out in 1189, now caused Sicily to lose many skilled artisans and merchants, as well as some of the most industrious farmers. Areas which had been garden suburbs of Palermo were now depopulated. Those Arabs who could not migrate fled to the hill country and joined the bandit groups of the interior. Although some of the refugees eventually returned and were even employed by the monarchy, confidence and trust between the Moslems and the Christians was never fully restored.

Also, in 1190, still during Tancred's reign, a major problem had developed when the king of England, Richard the Lionhearted, visited the island accompanied by the king of France and an army of crusaders. King Richard had come to demand the return of his sister Joanna's dowry. Joanna was the widow of the Sicilian-Norman monarch, William II, and Richard asserted that she and her dowry were being held illegally by Tancred. The English stayed for six months during which time many incidents occurred between the crusaders and the island's population. Trouble was especially frequent at Messina where the soldiers claimed that the Messinese merchants had been cheating them. The Sicilians, in turn, complained that the English had been accosting local women. Richard himself was involved in some violent incidents in Messina and, in retaliation against its citizens, sacked the city and burned its fleet. The French and English then occupied Messina for a month, forcing Tancred to buy peace. Tancred, at this time of course, needed help against his German rivals. Once peace was bought, Richard gave Tancred what was claimed to be King Arthur's famous sword, "Excalibur," as a gift, and then left for the crusades.

Certainly, by this time, Norman authority in the kingdom had greatly diminished. The King of Sicily was no longer an equal to the kings of France and England. And, he had even lost to the Pope more of the privileges attached to the Apostolic Legateship. Realizing all of this, and coveting the wealth of the island, Henry was now determined to invade and press forth his and his wife Constance's royal claims. This was made easier in 1194 by the death of Tancred. Henry immediately came to the island and, as has been noted, on Christmas Day at Palermo that same year, was crowned King of Sicily. His wife Constance, however, through whom he had inherited the royal title, was not present. She was detained in the town of Jesi in Apulia waiting for the birth of her child. Constance was aged forty and until that time had been childless. Determined that there should be no doubt about the child's authenticity, she assembled a group of nineteen cardinals and bishops, as well as numerous other courtiers and officials, to witness the royal birth in a huge tent that had been erected in the town square. On 26 December she gave birth to a son who was christened Frederick. There was cause for optimism, as the dynasty now had an heir.

But in Sicily, the harshness of Henry's policies soon made him most hated. Henry was a brilliant and ruthless man who was determined to establish his authority over all of Germany and Italy, from the North Sea to the African Straits, and turn it into a hereditary possession of his family. But the Sicilians, who for so long had been ruled by local dynasties that had always taken account of the needs of the island and its people, resisted.

Henry had also been ruthless towards the family of his rival claimant, Tancred. The immediate family of that former king all had died while being held captive by Henry, while all other supporters were brutally exterminated. Once Henry gained control of Sicily he left his wife as regent but put the power of the government in the hands of a German seneschal. Constance protested and in 1197 a plot to murder Henry was uncovered. There was some evidence that both Constance and the Pope were aware of the conspiracy. Henry suppressed this attempted plot with more brutality than before, but in a few months he was himself to die from an attack of dysentery or malaria, possibly caught while hunting in the marshes.

But Henry's death in 1197 did not bring peace to the island.

Although his widow did take over the government and replaced the German officials with native ones, her authority was insecure. Fortunately, however, she had a friend in the Pope, Innocent III. One of the most powerful and energetic of the medieval popes, Innocent was the guardian of Constance's son Frederick. The queen had been in poor health and had arranged the papal guardianship before her death in 1198. That year, her son Frederick, at the age of three, was crowned King of Sicily.

Frederick II, the new King of Sicily and through his father also, German Emperor, was on his father's side a Hohenstaufen from Swabia, but through his mother was a Norman and the grandson of the great Roger II. His childhood was spent in the exotic and cosmopolitan royal court at Palermo, but the years of his minority were often turbulent and difficult both for the young monarch and for the Sicilian kingdom. Frederick's guardian, Pope Innocent III, tried to control the kingdom and there were constant struggles between the chancellors and regents that Henry left to administer the realm until Frederick came of age. There were also renewed Moslem uprisings on the island. Girgenti was seized by the Moslem rebels and a large area near Monreale would be under their control. Their bases were in the hill country among bandit groups that had also settled there. When Frederick took over the government in 1208 at the age of fourteen he was faced with a kingdom that had been greatly impoverished. Royal territories had been given away by the Pope or were now occupied by feudal nobles. The new reign also began with a large debt owed to the Papacy and it was only through gifts from the cities that Frederick would have enough money to begin his administration.

But in time, under Frederick, Sicily regained some of its former glory. The island was his most beloved possession and he always considered the beautiful palace at Palermo to be his home. The court was centered there, and although the distractions of government would take him more and more away from the island, Frederick made sure that Sicily was provided with a just and orderly government. It was one of his administrators for Sicily, Peter della Vigna, who developed the *Liber Augustalis,* a codification of previous legal systems that had been in use on the island at various times. Instead of the diverse law codes for the different ethnic groups that had been used by the Norman rulers, this new system was uniform and emphasized the central authority of the monarch. Certain of the new laws are quite interesting. The wearing of swords was allowed only to royal servants. Strict penalties for blasphemers, frequenters of taverns, and adulterers were introduced, and a license and university degree were required to practice medicine. The code also included many enlightened provisions guaranteeing personal liberties.

Frederick was vigorous in the interest of the development of his imperial authority. Self government by the cities was not allowed and in each of the main centers, such as Palermo and Messina, as well as at strategic points throughout the island, large castles were built. These fortresses were not intended as royal residences but as military strongholds needed to uphold the royal power. Revolts by the cities, especially one at Messina in 1232, were ruthlessly suppressed. This subjugation of the towns ensured that there would not be an independent mercantile or professional class strong enough to challenge the authority of the landed aristocracy. But that, in time, would become a factor in an eventual political and economic decline on the island. Then, later, foreign cities, such as Pisa, Genoa, Amalfi, Lucca, and Venice would begin to dominate Sicilian trade. Frederick's intentions were, of course, the opposite. He had hoped to stimulate trade, agriculture, and industry and had planned his policies with that in mind.

One of the industries that Frederick encouraged was silk production, and here he was successful in reintroducing the experts needed to stimulate that important part of the economy. Besides the building of royal castles, Frederick undertook another revolutionary and controversial military policy that was aimed at strengthening the royal authority in the kingdom. This was the transportation of various populations to the mainland. Whole groups of people were moved about to repopulate different areas. The island of Malta was resettled. In Sicily, Lombards and Greeks were brought in to settle underpopulated various areas. But, there still had occurred, during the early years of Frederick's reign, several Arab uprisings. Frederick was not opposed to the Sicilian Arabs because of their Moslem faith, but because they had rebelled. After suppressing these rebellions, he ordered large Arab populations to be resettled on the mainland. Many thousands of Arabs were reestablished at Lucera, near Foggia, where they formed the basis for one of Frederick's military settlements. In fact, Lucera became the headquarters of his professional army which now consisted of large Moslem units. And, at Frederick's own royal court there were so many Moslem servants and officials that his opponent's referred to him as a "baptized Sultan."

Frederick was actually a most interesting and controversial figure of the age. He spoke Italian, French, German, Arabic, Latin, and Greek and in his youth he was known especially for his charm and fine appearance. Because of his energy, drive, and talents he would later come to be known as *Stupor Mundi*—"the Wonder of the World." Nowhere is this demonstrated more clearly than in the many scientific and cultural achievements made during his reign and under his personal auspices. While Frederick's personal patronage inclined more to science than to art the arts too, and especially literature, would flourish during this period. His inquisitive mind made him study the works of Jewish and Moslem, as well as Christian philosophers. Frederick even sent out surveys to try to learn how non-Christians regarded such beliefs as immortality and the existence of the soul. Because of his broadminded approach in these areas, quite uncharacteristic of his times, Frederick was accused by some Christians of keeping magicians and wizards at his court and of practicing such atrocities as isolating young children from any human contact to see what language they would come to speak on their own. He was also accused of dissecting living men to study the process of digestion.

Late in life Frederick published a scholarly and innovative treatise, *The Art of Falconry,* the result of his years of study of the breeding and training of that favorite royal bird. This work is filled with specific facts and technical details about the feeding and care of falcons, and also presents theories regarding their anatomy, flight patterns, and nesting habits. In it, Frederick also reveals himself to be a student of the classics, as he challenges the accounts of such authorities as Aristotle when they contradicted his own reason and observations. This interest in falcons was matched by an interest in other animals and Frederick maintained a private menagerie that included various exotic creatures. He took it with him wherever he traveled. His interest in zoology also led him to introduce new breeds of horses to Sicily. He was involved in the other sciences too, including mathematics, and one of his prized possessions was a miniature planetarium sent to him by the Sultan of Damascus. Among the learned men at Frederick's court were a noted Egyptian mathematician, al-Hanfi; the Italian, Leonardo Fibonacci; a Greek scientist, Theodore; and a Scotsman, Michael Scot who was an astrologer, philosopher, zoologist, and translator. Because he was considered also a wizard and magician, Scot appears in Dante's *Inferno* suffering the fate of a false prophet.

It was in the arts however, and especially in literature, that some of the most important achievements of the intellectual life of Frederick's court can be seen. It would be, in fact, at Frederick's court that the lyric form of poetry known as the sonnet was originally developed. Because Frederick's varied intellectual interests are the result of his early education at the cosmopolitan court of Palermo, it was therefore natural that he would take an interest in the development of a literature based on the Sicilian language. The spoken dialect of the island was not very different than that of today and it was most likely one of the languages that Frederick knew since childhood. Already, the literature of Provence had had an influence in Italy just as an Italian language and literature were being developed, and Palermo was one of the first places that the Provençal influence had appeared.

Through the wives of both William I and William II there had been connections with Provence, and many troubadours with their poetry also came with the invading forces of Richard the Lionhearted. Then in 1209, Frederick married Constance of Provence who brought with her more of the influence of that region. Under that influence, Sicilian vernacular poetry would develop. Dante and Petrarch have both acknowledged the preeminence of this Sicilian vernacular form and of it being the first Italian literary language.

The most noted proponents of what is termed the Sicilian School of poetry and was developed at Frederick's court were three individuals: Giacomo da Lentino, Rinaldo d'Aquino, and Pier della Vigna. Da Lentino, who is considered to be the author of the very first sonnet, was born near Syracuse. And, Rinaldo d'Aquino, who may have been a brother of Thomas Aquinas, also wrote a number of sonnets as well as *canzoni,* a type of lyric poem that developed out of the songs of the common people. Pier della Vigna served also as an influential minister of Frederick's. He held important and sensitive diplomatic and administrative posts, and was one of the most noted statesmen of the time. But, because of the jealousy of other courtiers, he was falsely implicated in a plot against the Emperor who, being prone to deal cruelly with any who defied him, imprisoned della Vigna. The poet's subsequent brutal death, possibly a suicide, underlines the negative aspect of Frederick's nature. Della Vigna too, is immortalized in Dante.

Frederick's reputation also was made in war and in politics and, besides suppressing various rebellions in Germany and various parts of Italy, he also undertook a crusade. Known for his indifference to religion, Frederick's interest in the cause of the crusades was purely political. While he was in many ways an opponent of the Papacy and had even been excommunicated, he undertook the crusade to gain control of the Middle East and extend his own influence and power. It was by marriage to his second wife, Yolanda of Brienne, the heiress of the Kingdom of Jerusalem, that Frederick had a claim to Middle Eastern territory. Through a treaty with the Sultan of Egypt, he gained Palestine, and in 1229 crowned himself King of Jerusalem.

The Holy Land was taken without bloodshed, but Frederick's subsequent high handed behavior soon made him hated throughout his new kingdom.

Back in Europe in 1235, his own son, Henry, led a rebellion against Frederick who, in turn, quickly bribed officials in Germany to betray Henry and then had him imprisoned. Although he was in time released, Henry was deprived of his authority and died in a riding accident in 1242. Frederick's next years were spent involved in the wars taking place among the Italian city states, especially those in the Lombard League. These wars were fought to determine whether the cities would be under the authority of the Papacy or the German Emperor, in this case, Frederick. The terms "Guelph" and "Ghibelline" first appeared at this time and refering respectively to the supporters of the papal and the imperial causes. Then, in 1251, Frederick died. The papacy rejoiced over the death of this Emperor who was both great and cruel, while for Sicily it meant the beginning of a new period of strife, as various factions again contested the right to rule the island.

Frederick had left behind several children, legitimate and illegitimate, but he passed on the Kingdom of Sicily to his eldest legitimate son to whom it was due by hereditary right. However it took several years for this son, known as Conrad, to establish his claim over the many rival factions that had arisen after Frederick's death. For Sicily, this period marked the beginning of a long period of decline in power and prosperity. Palermo, for instance, with the absence of the royal court, would cease to be the political, artistic, and commercial center that it had been under Frederick, and many creative individuals soon left.

Conrad himself arrived in Sicily only later, as he had to spend the early years of his reign pacifying the rest of his Italian territories. During that time, Sicily was ruled by his loyal governor, Peter Ruffo. The Papacy however, would not recognize Conrad's claims as the Pope, before Frederick's death, had named a pretender, William of Holland to the throne. The nomination of a new claimant by the Pope was permitted under feudal law because the Pope was the overlord of the king of Sicily and because Frederick had been excommunicated. Also, the Papacy did not want to see the union of the Sicilian kingdom with Germany. War was now inevitable, but before that happened Conrad, in 1254, fell ill and died at age 26. On his deathbed he named his son Conrad II, also known as Conradin, to the throne of Sicily. This two-year old boy was the only living legitimate prince of the Hohenstaufen line.

But the Pope, Innocent IV, refused to act as guardian for the child or to support his claims to the island. Instead, he decided to rule the Kingdom of Sicily directly. The Pope had the support of Peter Ruffo and John the Moor, the commander of the Arab divisions of the Hohenstaufen army. Both believed that the young Conradin's claims would be difficult to uphold and anyway the boy was not considered to have been completely disinherited—he was still recognized by all parties as the King of Jerusalem. In fact, at this time most of the Hohenstaufen supporters were quickly joining the side of another claimant, Manfred, an older illegitimate son of Frederick's who claimed to have been legitimized before his father's death.

At this point, the Pope changed his mind and agreed that Conradin's claims could be recognized when he came of age, but in the meantime the kingdom was to be administered by the Papacy. Manfred could be recognized as "balio" or governor of the island. Apparently, neither Manfred nor the Pope really intended to honor the arrangement. Then shortly after, upon Pope Innocent's death, a new pope, Alexander IV, renewed the papacy's earlier quarrel with Manfred. Pope Alexander began a search for a new foreign prince to take over the Sicilian realm. Manfred by now, however, was supreme in southern Italy and in 1255, after his victory over the papal army, the Church recognized Conradin's claim to Sicily with Manfred acting as regent. By 1257, Manfred had control of the island and, having gained support among various sections of the population, now threw off the pretext of ruling for Conradin and had himself crowned King of Sicily at Palermo. He was 26 years of age.

Having inherited the charming personality of his father, Manfred, who was actually unscrupulous and cruel, was able to make others overlook his defects. Described by the poet Dante as a handsome, blond monarch, Manfred had his father's love of learning, and was even more skillful in placating his opposition than Frederick had been. Had he been content in ruling in the style of his Norman ancestors, peacefully governing the island and the southern mainland and restricting his activities to schemes that would have benefited his subjects, he might have founded a lasting dynasty. But, after his coronation, Manfred seldom visited Sicily and the kingdom's talent and money followed him north where he had become involved in territorial and political ambitions. In time, Sicily became a mere appendix to the mainland.

Nor was Manfred concerned about Germany, as very few of the subjects there recognized the claims of the young prince Conradin, who Manfred was supposed to be representing. Then, in 1256, the rival candidate, William of Holland, who had been put forth by the Papacy, died. However, the choice of imperial candidate traditionally had to be ratified by the seven Prince-Electors of the German Empire. In 1257, they split their votes and chose two candidates for the throne. Four of the electors chose Richard of Cornwall, the brother of King Henry of England. Then, because one of the electors changed his vote, Alfonso X, King of Castile, also received four votes. Both factions wanted a wealthy foreign prince with no connections to the Hohenstaufens. But, in the end, neither of these claimants actually would be crowned emperor.

Meanwhile, in Italy, many Hohenstaufen supporters, angered at Manfred's usurpation of the Sicilian throne, seemed ready to give their support to Conradin. Manfred's armies, however, had by this time, overrun much of the papal territory, the papal power being dissipated in the ongoing struggles between the Guelph and Ghibelline cities in Italy. He soon controlled most of the peninsula. But, whoever rules in Sicily and southern Italy must also pay attention to what is happening in the neighboring territories just across the sea, and the kings of Sicily always had to have a particular interest in the affairs of North Africa and the Byzantine state. Manfred was not interested in power in North Africa but he did take advantage of divisions within the Byzantine Empire and became involved in the tangled web of affairs in that realm. He sent his armies to Greece and, as a result of these campaigns, was able to increase his resources and also gained a wife, Helena of Epirus. By 1258, Manfred would be at the height of his power.

At that time however, a new Pope, Urban III, was elected. He had as his first priority the restoration of the papal lands taken by Manfred. The Pope's ultimate goal was to really to drive Manfred from southern Italy and Sicily. According to feudal tradition, the King of Sicily was the Pope's vassal. As such, he could in theory be deposed by the Pope and a new king loyal to the Papacy could be appointed in his place. The Popes, of course, had always realized this, but they first needed a prince strong enough and willing to take on the war that would be needed to remove Manfred. With this in mind, the Pope offered the crown of Sicily to an English prince, Edmund, who was the younger son of King Henry III. For this great honor there was a price. A huge sum was supposed to be collected in England and sent to Rome for the war against Manfred. Edmund was duly invested in England with the title of King of Sicily and Henry III proceeded to collect the monies promised. However, the amount was so large that he was unable to make the payment. Then,

In 1262, a new Pope Urban IV, a Frenchman, offered the kingdom of Sicily to Charles of Anjou who was the brother of Saint Louis, the King of France. Charles had both the means and determination to take Sicily and southern Italy from Manfred. He accepted the terms of the papal offer, which included renouncing any claim to the Apostolic Legateship of Sicily, and set about expanding his power and influence in preparation for a war with Manfred. In 1265, Charles began his invasion of Italy and, by the end of that year, was in control of several territories in the south. He and his wife had already been crowned at Rome as rulers of Sicily. Early in 1266, Charles's forces met Manfred's at Benevento in Campania. Before the battle Charles was supposed to have said: "Tell the Sultan of Lucera (Manfred) for me that today I will send him to hell, or he will send me to paradise." In a fierce and brutal battle Manfred was slain and his army defeated. Charles of Anjou made a triumphal entry into Naples, ready to claim the crown of southern Italy and Sicily. The memory of Manfred meanwhile, would live on in Sicilian folklore as the story of a heroic prince who had tried to defend the island against the forces of both the Papacy and the French. Sicilian history would again enter another phase as a new dynasty, the Angevin, had now come to rule on the island.

"Pantokrator" Mosaic, Monreale Cathedral. Founded by the Norman king William in 1174, the Cathedral of Monreale splendidly combines Byzantine, Arabic, and Norman elements. Its grandeur is especially revealed in its interior mosaics, especially the Christ "Pantokrator," done in the Byzantine style. Covering an area over 6,000 sq. meters, the mosaics are second in size only to those of St. Sophia in Constantinople.

Mosaic, Norman Royal Palace, Palermo. The Arabic influence in Sicily is evident in the orange and date trees depicted in this mosaic from the Royal Palace in Palermo. These fruits were first brought to the island in the 7th century by the Arabs.

Castle of Ziza, Palermo. Built on the site of the Emir's Palace, the castle of Ziza was enlarged in the 12th century by the Normans who called in Byzantine and Arab artists to adorn the building. Its name is derived from the Arabic "aziz," meaning "marvel." (Courtesy of New York Public Library Picture Collection.)

Sarcophagus of Emperor Frederick II, Palermo Cathedral. Known as "Stupor Mundi"—"the Wonder of the World," the Hohenstaufen Emperor Frederick II (1198–1250) was one of the most fascinating and controversial rulers of his age. A brilliant patron of literature, and the arts, and sciences, he made his cosmopolitan court at Palermo a center of 13th century culture and learning. (Courtesy of New York Public Library Picture Collection.)

VIII
The Sicilian Vespers

IN 1268, THE NEW FRENCH RULER OF SICILY, CHARLES OF ANJOU, WHO
had defeated Manfred of Hohenstaufen, was challenged by the other
claimant for the Sicilian throne, Conradin, the sixteen year old son of
the former king, Conrad II. With the encouragement of the Papacy,
Charles began a war against Conradin and his supporters in Italy.
Conradin, in turn, issued a proclamation that he alone was the
legitimate heir of the Hohenstaufens. This young and popular prince
was enthusiastically welcomed into Rome by the population before
he set out to conquer his kingdom in the south. Finally, these two
rival claimants and their armies met at the battle of Tagliacozzo.
There, Conradin's forces were completely defeated and he was taken
prisoner. Captured with Conradin was his friend and political ally,
Frederick of Baden, another young prince who, like Conradin had
been disinherited of his own kingdom in Germany.

Charles of Anjou feared Conradin, not only because he had a
claim on the Sicilian kingdom, but also because he was a charming
and popular youth, with many followers. The Anjou claimant knew
that his own position would never be secure so long as Conradin
lived. To murder a royal prince, captured after a bravely fought
battle, however, would be a gross violation of the medieval code of
chivalry and honor. To justify such an act, Charles had his lawyers
prepare an indictment declaring Conradin's invasion to be an act of
robbery and treason. With this, both Conradin and his friend
Frederick were condemned to death by beheading. Although Charles
acted to secure his throne, he committed an act of judicial murder
that would mar his name for centuries to come.

Charles's two military victories in Italy ensured that he would now
control his southern Italian and Sicilian kingdom. Once he and his
wife had been crowned at Rome as rulers of Sicily, he set out to make
himself the greatest king in Europe. He was known to be notoriously

ambitious and severe, with little sense of humor, although he it was said that he could be magnanimous to his supporters. The medieval chronicler Villani wrote that not even the minstrels wept when he died.

Like every invader of Sicily, Charles at first did find some support among the people. The inhabitants, always resentful of the policies and taxes of their governments, were ready to help each new foreign ruler in the hope that conditions would improve. However, as soon as that new ruler tried to finance the costs of his invasion and reward his followers and army with Sicilian lands, the people would rebel all over again. Actually, the population was often divided against itself and different cities and families would try to use the change in government to their own advantage. Messina and Syracuse, for instance, at first helped the French forces to subdue the rest of the island.

Charles's troops were really a group of adventurers and mercenaries whose intention was to plunder and loot as they conquered the kingdom. Charles himself did not come to Sicily to lead the invasion, nor did he even visit the island after the conquest. Thus, he ignored the honored tradition by which the king was chosen and acclaimed by the barons and citizens at Palermo. His real intention was to use the kingdom for his larger ambitions for a Mediterranean empire. He therefore had to weaken the sense of independence and cohesion that the previous Norman rulers had so much helped to develop on the island. Charles also brought religious intolerance into a society that had, in fact, flourished because of tolerance. And, his commanders soon earned a reputation for cruelty as subdued resistance on the island.

But, in a sense, the French were probably really not much more arbitrary and brutal than previous conquerors. The difference was that now, because there were other interests, conflict was more difficult to avoid. Large estates were confiscated as payment to the invaders who had helped Charles secure the kingdom and foreign officials replaced Sicilians in chief administrative posts in the cities and districts. Angevin rule in Sicily began to resemble that of an armed camp ruling a resentful territory. Also, Charles centered the court and the public and social life of the kingdom at Naples. Sicily was pushed to the background. In all the years of his reign, Charles would visit the island only once, on a stopover from his campaigns in Tunis. No parliament would ever meet in Sicily during his rule.

However, Charles's administration of the island was, in some ways, efficient and even profitable for trade. The tax system was reorganized and commerce with the mainland, especially Naples, increased. But this efficiency also served to increase the resentment against the new rulers. It was coupled with a resentment that was also felt because of the lack of regard for local traditions, as well as an attitude of aloofness and indifference towards the island's problems, that also came to characterize Angevin rule.

By 1282, Charles had made himself, through his conquests, the greatest potentate in Europe. He was King of Sicily, Jerusalem and Albania, ruler of Provence and other French territories, regent in Greece and overlord of Tunis. But he still was ambitious, and for some time had been planning an even bigger campaign—the conquest of the Byzantine Empire. He hoped to become the greatest Mediterranean ruler since the Byzantine emperor Justinian. But he seemed to have forgotten that he had very dissatisfied and restless subjects in Sicily and enemies elsewhere in Europe who were sworn to his destruction.

Among these enemies was Peter I, ruler of the Spanish kingdom of Aragon. Peter was married to Constance, the daughter of Manfred of Hohenstaufen. To many, she was the legitimate and true heir to the Kingdom of Sicily. King Peter's court at Barcelona became a refuge for many of the exiles who had left Sicily because of their opposition to the Angevin regime. Among these exiles was a certain John of Procida who had served as both an advisor and physician to Frederick II and, upon his death, had entered the service of Manfred. In exile at the court of Aragon, he rose to become King Peter I's Chancellor, a position granted to him in recognition of both of his learning and his loyalty to the House of Hohenstaufen. While at the court, John of Procida maintained a contact with many of Charles's enemies and, when Charles's planned campaign against the Eastern Empire became known, John quickly began negotiations with the Byzantine Emperor Michael. A conspiracy aimed at thwarting Charles's political ambitions was organized. The plot was to have three centers, Aragon, Constantinople, and most importantly, Sicily itself. Gold and agents would be sent to Sicily from the two royal courts to help organize an uprising that was to coincide with the sailing of the Aragonese fleet. Circumstances, however, would cause events to turn out somewhat differently.

In the year 1282, Easter Monday, a holiday, fell on March 30. Throughout the preceding day, all of Sicily had been calm. The Angevin fleet was anchored at Messina and supplies were being collected throughout the island for the expedition against Constantinople. The Sicilian countryside was controlled from 42 castles, but the troops stationed there to watch the population noticed nothing out of the ordinary. The people, of course, always showed a resentment to the foreign forces, but this had become typical and was even expected.

Just outside of Palermo, on the river Oreto, stands the church of the Holy Spirit. It had been dedicated in 1177 by the English-born archbishop of the city, Walter Offamil, or "of the Mill," and it was customary for Easter Monday celebrations, culminating in the Vesper service, to be held there. A large crowd had gathered and, while talking and singing, noticed the appearance of a group of French officials who had come to join the festivities. They were greeted coldly, but persisted in mingling with the crowd. Some began to approach the younger women with a familiarity that angered the Sicilians. Then, a French sergeant named Drouet took a young married woman apart from the crowd, annoying her with his attentions. Her husband, outraged, drew a knife and stabbed Drouet to death. As the other Frenchmen rushed to avenge their comrade they too were surrounded by hostile men, all armed with swords and daggers. A struggle ensued out of which none of the French survived. At this point the church bell, and all the church bells of the city, began to ring for Vespers.

It was to the sound of these Vesper bells that messengers ran through the streets calling on the men of Palermo to rise up against the foreign oppressor. With cries of *moranu li franchiski* ("death to the French" in the Sicilian dialect), they ran into the houses and inns frequented by the French and slaughtered every Frenchman and every woman who had married a Frenchman that they could find. French convents and monasteries were also raided and anyone who could not pronounce correctly the word "ciciri," whose sound was difficult for the French to enunciate, was slain. The leading French official, the Justiciar of Palermo, John of Saint-Rémy, barely escaped the violence and, with a few followers, fled to a castle in the interior.

The next day the rebels were in complete control of Palermo. Now, they had to consider the future. The city was proclaimed an independent Commune and a leading Sicilian knight, Roger Mastangelo, was elected leader. The Angevin flag was taken down and replaced with the imperial Hohenstaufen eagle. Then, a message was sent to the Pope asking him to take the Palermo Commune under his protection.

Meanwhile, news of the uprising had spread to other parts of the island. Messengers had already gone out to all the towns and villages telling the people to strike first against the oppressors before they themselves were struck down. The Justiciar of Palermo was finally captured in his castle and, with his guards, killed. During the week, news came of similar uprisings and of the massacre of the French elsewhere on the island. The first to follow the example of Palermo was the town of Corleone, which also proclaimed itself a Commune. Together, these two Communes sent troops out in three directions: west to Trapani, south towards Caltanissetta, and east to Messina. The troops were to alert the rest of the island and coordinate a full scale rebellion. In each district, as these soldiers approached, the French were either massacred or they fled. Only in two towns were they spared. In one, Calatafimi, because the leading Angevin official, William Porcelet, was beloved by the people for his benevolence and sense of justice, he and his family were spared and allowed to embark for Provence. In the other town, Sperlinga, there was no uprising because that community had always prided itself on its independence and separateness from the rest of the island. There, the French garrison was allowed to retreat safely to Messina.

In Messina itself there was no immediate uprising. A strong French garrison was stationed in the city while in the harbor was the Angevin fleet. Moreover, Messina was the center of Charles's government in Sicily and certain leading families there had benefited from the support that he had given to that city.

Two weeks after the rebellion had started, the Commune of Palermo sent a message to the citizens of Messina asking them to join in the revolt. In response, the governor of Messina, Herbert of Orléans, sent seven galleys to blockade Palermo's harbor. But in Messina opinion was now turning in favor of the revolt. There were many natives of Palermo living in Messina who had relocated to that city when it had been made the administrative center of the island. At this point, the French governor decided to make sure that all was under control in his district. He sent a garrison of Frenchmen under the command of a Neapolitan, Micheletto Gatta, to occupy nearby Taormina and replace the Messinese garrison that had been stationed there. Instead, the Messinese commander, William Chiriolo, fought the French troops and took them prisoner. Two days later, Messina rose up in revolt. The French were expelled and a Commune was proclaimed headed by a leading citizen, Baldwin Mussone. The Angevin officials were allowed to leave for France in two ships, but when one of these broke the agreement and sailed for Naples to join King Charles, the Messinese were so angry that they intercepted the other vessel and threw everyone overboard.

The leader of the Messina Commune was assisted in his administration by a committee of four that included Raynald of Limogia, Peter Ansalano, Nicholas Saporito, and Bartholomew of Neocastro, who later wrote a history of the Vespers. It was decided at this point to send news of the uprising to Constantinople and alert the Byzantine Emperor Michael that a blow had been struck against his enemy King Charles. It was hoped that the Byzantines would send more funds to help the growing revolt on the island. Later, in his memoirs, the Emperor claimed that he was instrumental in helping the Sicilians overthrow the Angevin rule and in thwarting Charles's plans for an expedition to the East, saving his own empire from destruction.

When King Charles first got news of the revolt back in Naples, he did not consider it to be serious and was merely annoyed that he might have to postpone his expedition to the East. It was only after he learned of the uprising in Messina and of the subsequent destruction of his fleet in the harbor that he understood how much had been lost. "Lord God," he cried, "since it has pleased You to ruin my fortune, let me only go down by small steps." In his rage he was said to have gnawed at his scepter, while swearing to reduce the island to a desolate desert as warning to any who would dare to rebel against him. He then set about to cancel the great expedition and prepare his forces to retake Sicily. At this point, a Sicilian friar came to him seeking an audience. Charles asked how he dared to come to him from "that land of traitors." The friar bravely replied that he was not a traitor nor was Sicily a land of traitors. Instead, he answered, it was Charles who had abandoned the people committed by God to his care. Now, they were simply avenging the wrongs done to them, and were willing to die in defense of their rights. The friar, surprisingly, was allowed to leave unharmed. Charles may have been impressed by his bravery, or he may have wanted a report to get back to the island telling just how formidable the invasion force he had prepared would be. Of course, offers of reform were also made to the Sicilians by Charles, but the people were unmoved. The Angevin rule had caused too much resentment to ever again be trusted. The Sicilians, especially the Messinese, had instead already made preparations for the King's counter-attack.

A new commander, Alaimo of Lentini, who had originally been part of John of Procida's conspiracy to start a revolution on the island, was selected as the leader of the Messina Commune. Aliamo's wife, Machalda of Scaletta, who herself would later play a controversial role in the intrigues following the revolt, had already led a force to Catania where she fooled the French garrison there into surrendering to the Messinese forces and then took control herself of the city.

In August, Charles made his first attack against Messina, but was driven back by Alaimo's troops. Later, the French tried a night attack but were discovered through the efforts of two local women, known merely as Dina and Clarentia. They later became famous in the history of the revolt as the heroines who saved their city from that sudden assault. Today, figures representing these two heroines can be seen in the city's famous animated clock tower. Really, all the citizens, under the command of Alaimo, took part in the defense of Messina. An appeal had been made to the Papacy to take the city under its protection, but the Pope would agree only if its citizens surrendered to Charles. When the papal legate came with such an answer, the Commune's officials took back the keys to the city that symbolically had been placed in his hands as a sign of good faith, and asked him to leave. Charles meanwhile, had sent a personal offer of a pardon and a bribe of several large estates if Alaimo would surrender the city, but this was contemptuously rejected by the commander.

By this time, delegates from the Communes of Sicily had been meeting also met with King Peter of Aragon. Peter agreed to lead an invasion but, as a pretense, ostensibly prepared his fleet for a crusade against North Africa. There, he told the Sicilian envoys, he would instead establish a base from which he could invade the island and come to the aid of the rebels. The envoys told him that the people already considered his wife, Constance, to be the lawful Hohenstaufen heir to the kingdom. At the end of August, 1282, Aragonese forces, led by Peter, invaded Sicily, coming ashore near Trapani. With the king came an army of 600 mounted knights and 8,000 *almugaveri,* guerrilla infantry known for their ferocity in battle. The Sicilian revolt had become a war.

Of course, the first massacre at Palermo on Easter Monday of what came to be known as the "Sicilian Vespers" and the subsequent uprising at Messina had been the work of the Sicilian people themselves. They had acted spontaneously and unknowingly ahead of the schedule that had been set for an uprising by John of Procida and the Byzantine Emperor. According to that earlier plan, the revolt was to have taken place only after the Aragonese fleet had landed to assist the rebels. Thus, although the Sicilians had received preliminary funds for the revolt, they alone had done the early fighting. But now, they had an ally in the King of Aragon.

Peter of Aragon proceeded to Palermo where he was acclaimed by the Commune as king of Sicily. Then, after immediately swearing to restore on the island the laws and traditions of the "Good King William," he set out with his army and forces from Palermo towards

Messina. Envoys were sent ahead to Charles to present Peter's claims to the kingdom. Charles rejected these claims and, not wishing to be caught between an unconquered city and an approaching army, he moved his forces across the Straits and made camp in Calabria. Peter made a triumphal and uncontested entry into Messina.

On his way to that city, King Peter had had an unusual experience. An old beggar, who claimed that he had been a friend of King Manfred, said that he had come to warn Peter of the treachery of Alaimo and his wife, Machalda. Peter thought little of this until the next evening. His forces had paused at the village of Santa Lucia before going on to Messina and it was there that he was met by Machalda. She had a plan to seduce the king and become the royal mistress. It was only by protestations of his devotion to his wife that King Peter extricated himself from this embarrassing situation. The result of this encounter was that Machalda would form a jealous hatred of Queen Constance, and would now use her influence on her husband Alaimo to draw him into plots against the House of Aragon.

But, for the moment, Alaimo was unmoved and welcomed Peter into Messina as the liberator of the island. A joint Sicilian and Aragonese force soon set out to attack the Angevin forces in Calabria. Peter, by now in control of Sicily, landed on the Italian mainland near Nicastro. Because this landing site was at the narrowest point of land in central Calabria, in the "toe" of the Italian "boot," Charles and his army, at there base in Reggio, were cut off from the rest of the mainland. Naples remained under the control of Charles's son, who is known as Charles of Salerno. Once this war came to Italy, it became part also of the struggle going on between the Guelph and Ghibelline factions in the Italian cities. The Ghibellines, it will be remembered, generally represented the supporters of the imperial, or Hohenstaufen cause. In this conflict they sided, of course, with King Peter. The Guelphs, or supporters of papal supremacy, generally stood with the Pope's ally King Charles. At any event, by winter, the war came to a stalemate.

The conflict had also wasted the resources of both kings. The foreign policy of both Aragon and the House of Anjou had become costly and, as the war for Sicily continued, the resources of both sides were being depleted. This dread of a long and costly war helps to explain an unusual proposal that Charles made at the end of 1282. He proposed that the possession of the kingdom of Sicily be decided by a single combat between the two kings. Peter quickly agreed but, after some reflection, both sides modified the proposal to a combat between each king leading a force of one hundred knights. The day of the contest was set for June 1, 1283. It was to take place at the neutral site of Bordeaux, then the capital of the French domains of the king of England. Of course, fellow rulers throughout Europe were generally skeptical about the proposed duel, and felt that, while it was part of the medieval tradition, it was also a somewhat obsolete way to reach a political decision. But, as both Charles and Peter had already consented, they could not very well back out without losing face.

In the first months of 1283, Charles moved his forces towards France where he intended to meet with his nephew, King Philip. His son, Charles of Salerno, was left as regent in Calabria. There, from his camp at San Martino, the younger Charles summoned a parliament to meet and offer to the people of Sicily certain reforms. A promise was made to restore the laws of the "Good King William." But, again the Sicilians were unmoved. They now wanted complete independence from Angevin rule.

By early spring 1283, both Charles and Peter, with their knights, had arrived in France for the impending duel. However, although a date for the combat had been set, no one had named the hour. Early in the morning of June 1, King Peter and his knights rode out to the designated field of combat where they found themselves alone. King Peter's heralds announced his presence and, after waiting a short time, proclaimed that he had a victory by default. His opponent had failed to meet him. Later that same day, King Charles arrived on the field with his companions and followed the same procedure. He too, claimed a victory by default. In fact, each king had found a way to save face and proclaim a victory without entering into the ill-conceived combat. Apparently, this had been prearranged after each monarch realized the foolhardiness of the original proposal. Now, they were free to continue the war in earnest and on a much larger scale.

Meanwhile, Queen Constance of Aragon, the Hohenstaufen heiress of Sicily, had already arrived on the island where she was acting as regent for her husband. She soon had to be concerned with the restlessness of the Almogavar mercenaries who had been part of Peter's early invasion force. These troops had been very effective but had now had begun to plunder and loot throughout the island. Also, there was some dissatisfaction among the Sicilian rebels themselves. They had seen the Spanish as allies, coming to help liberate Sicily. Now, it seemed that the Spanish might only be another conqueror, come to take control of the island while ignoring the wishes of the

Sicilian people. Among these dissatisfied rebels was Alaimo di Lentini.

At the same time, the combined Aragonese and Sicilian fleets, under the command of the brilliant admiral, Roger of Lauria, won a major victory over the French. After the mock "combat" between the kings at Bordeaux had taken place, Charles remained in France for a year, leaving the war in Sicily to be waged by his son, Charles of Salerno. Meanwhile, news of the Sicilian Vespers and Peter of Aragon's conquest of Sicily had inspired several revolts on the mainland. In Forlì, for instance, hundreds of French were massacred, and in Rome a similar revolt broke out against the French garrison that was stationed there.

Finally, at the end of 1284 Charles left France. He sailed south, proceeding cautiously so as not to come across the Aragonese fleet. Charles also told his son to avoid, at all costs, a naval encounter. But, not being as cautious as his father, the younger Charles let the Angevin fleet sail out of Naples and right into an encounter with Roger of Lauria's ships. The Angevin forces were decisively defeated and the regent himself was captured. When this debacle became known in Naples, anti-French rioting broke out there too. King Charles, when he got the news of what happened, had no pity for his captive son and exclaimed: "Who loses a fool loses nothing. Why is he not dead for disobeying us?" The young Charles soon was released as part of a hostage exchange, but he was deprived of all power by his angry father.

In Naples, King Charles arrested hundreds suspected of participating in the riots, and then made plans to continue the war. But, he was desperately pressed for money. His dreams of empire, were of course, by now gone and Peter of Aragon was in possession of most of the major sites in Calabria, including Reggio. Charles led a seige of that city, but gave up after two weeks as the Aragonese fleet was continuing to attack the Calabrian coast. The population there had, by now, no interest in fighting for the French and so the Aragonese forces never met any opposition when they landed. Charles retreated to Apulia for the winter. He had hoped to stay there and plan a new campaign for the coming spring, but he soon fell gravely ill. In January, 1285, he died. With his death, Angevin rule of Sicily had finally come to an end. Now, a new dynasty, the Spanish House of Aragon, would take control of the island, beginning a new phase in its history.

It is clear however, that, while many factions and groups had helped in expelling Angevin rule from the island, in the end it was the spirit of the Sicilian people, first demonstrated at the Vesper uprising at Palermo, that really liberated Sicily. The Spanish forces, the support of the Byzantine Emperor, and the brilliance of such commanders as Roger of Lauria, all helped to make the revolution possible, but the main credit must go to the Sicilians themselves. They alone provided the motive force for the revolt and had the determination to fight for their homeland. And, the Vespers uprising did more than just change the course of Sicilian history. The effects of this revolt fundamentally changed the history of Europe. Because of the uprising, one empire, the Byzantine, was saved, while another, that of Charles of Anjou, was ended. Moreover, the balance of power of the medieval Papacy was now totally altered.

Regarding Sicily itself, while the island would not be independent until the nineteenth century, when it was united with the newly formed Italian state, the Vespers would always serve as an inspiration in any of the later struggles of the Sicilian people against the tyrants who sought to rule their homeland.

IX

The House of Aragon

With the death of King Charles, Angevin power in Sicily ended and Peter of Aragon became the island's new ruler. Immediately, Peter realized that he had to quickly establish a basis of power and support because, although the Sicilians had welcomed his assistance, he did not have the absolute rights of a conqueror. Thus, his best hope was to be conciliatory toward the local feudal nobility and the population in general. As a first move, Peter restored Palermo to its former position of importance over Messina, the latter having been favored by the Angevins. Parliaments, which had never met under Charles, were again called and, at one of them, Peter agreed that the island would remain an entity separate from the Kingdom of Aragon. Sicily, he promised, would never be merged with that Spanish kingdom. To guarantee this, he designated that upon his death the two crowns would be held by separate individuals from his family.

But, many of the leaders of the Vesper rebellion were still dissatisfied. They had fought for independence and fair government and yet all of the old problems and grievances seemed to now be reemerging. Special feudal taxes that had been imposed under the Angevins were once again being collected, while the hereditary rights of the feudal nobility were largely ignored. Likewise, a new Spanish aristocracy was now being given land on the island, in effect replacing the original Norman-Sicilian barons. In response to this, some of these barons began again to plot and intrigue against the Spanish. Among them, was Alaimo di Lentini who, it will be remembered, originally had deserted Manfred for the cause of Charles, and then had betrayed Charles and joined the Spanish, from whom he obtained large estates. Now, he was plotting against the island's Spanish rulers.

As new rulers, the Spanish immediately recognized Sicily's commercial importance. Grains and finished products, especially silk, formed the basis for a lucrative trade with Catalonia, and soon it would be the Catalan merchants and bankers who benefited the most. Some of the trade between Sicily and North Africa was also transferred to Aragon. Also, because Peter had intended the conquest of Sicily to be a stepping stone to the eventual conquest of southern Italy, the Sicilian fleet was taken over by the Spanish for that purpose.

Peter, however, died less than a year after taking power and, despite his promises, Sicily was merged with Aragon under the rule of his eldest son, James. The new king simply ignored requests for Sicilian autonomy and, in fact, even had plans to make peace with the Pope, surrendering the island back to the Angevins. In effect, James would disregard the efforts of all who had struggled for independence since the time of the Vesper uprising in 1282. Of course, he met with great opposition.

James had as his Viceroy in Palermo his younger brother Frederick. But Frederick actually had been brought to Sicily as a young child and had been raised as a Sicilian. Thus, he very much identified with the island and its people. Probably, he had ambitions of his own, which would have been threatened by his brother James's proposal to surrender the island to the Pope and the Angevins. To counter this possibility, Frederick, in 1295, called the Sicilian parliament to debate the issue. The parliament decided that Frederick should become the king of an independent Sicily. He was supported in this position by the admiral Roger of Lauria, the famous victor over the Angevin fleet, and by John of Procida. Also, Frederick's fiancée, princess Catherine of Courtenay, was landless and told him that a princess without lands should not marry a prince who was also landless. So, Frederick was now determined to take the crown of Sicily. To support of him, the Sicilian barons had defied even the order of excommunication issued by the Pope. Even some of the Spanish barons now living and holding territory on the island backed Frederick, demonstrating that, by this time, they, too, had come to identify with the Sicilian nobility. In fact, neither the King of Aragon nor the Pope offered any real resistance, and this major change was accomplished without violence or bloodshed.

The new King of Sicily, now known as Frederick III, was crowned in 1296. He would rule for forty years, but this was to be a period of almost constant warfare against Angevin Naples and a most destructive period for the Sicilian kingdom. In time a new Pope proclaimed a crusade against King Frederick. But, Frederick, of course, was seeking to reestablish claims to the island based on the fact that he was the son of the Hohenstaufen heiress and therefore considered himself to be of that dynasty as well as of Norman lineage. He also wished to avenge the former Norman rulers, Manfred and Conradin. Because of his claims Frederick also had the support of the Ghibelline cities of Italy. But, his brother, King James, never recognized these claims and, in time, landed an army on the island and declared war. In 1298, some of the leading Sicilian barons too, deserted Frederick and joined the newly formed coalition of Naples, Aragon, and the papacy.

Frederick finally was forced to accept a compromise. In 1302, he agreed to a peace settlement in which he could keep the kingdom during his lifetime but, upon his death, it would pass to the Angevins. He had also to agree to accept the Pope as a feudal overlord, to grant special arrangements for the shipping of Sicilian grain to Rome, and to style himself only as King of Trinacria, the ancient name for Sicily. Actually, Frederick only agreed to these terms to buy time. He continued to call himself King of Sicily and, because he regarded the treaty as invalid, issued a declaration that any foreign treaty had to be ratified by the Sicilian parliament. In reality, Frederick had only agreed to the earlier terms because, by making a quick peace, he was able to save Sicily from the brutality of the mercenary troops who always accompanied invading forces. In fact, one of the most aggressive of these mercenary bands, the infamous "Catalan Company," had already left the island and moved east, conquering Athens and attaching it temporarily to the Sicilian kingdom.

However, in 1312, war began again. This time it would continue, intermittently, for the next sixty years. During that period, various coastal areas of Sicily were often in Angevin possession. This control, however, never extended to the interior where guerrilla bands successfully held the territory. Sometimes, Frederick's forces themselves even invaded the Italian mainland but, overall, the long war tended to wear down the Sicilian economy. Only the Sicilian barons gained in terms of power and influence during this period.

Frederick, of course, had to make concessions to the baronial class, and among these was the agreement to reserve the island's chief administrative posts for the barons. But, although he faced many difficulties as a ruler, Frederick III was generally considered to be generous and amiable. Like his ancestors, Roger II and Frederick II, he was cultivated and educated and respected by the writers and thinkers of his time. He was, for instance, a favorite of the poet

Dante's, especially because he defied the Pope. When Frederick III died in 1337, at least Sicily was still independent, but just barely.

King Frederick was succeeded by his son, Frederick IV. During his reign, the baronial houses of Chiaramonte and Ventimiglia began to dominate the island. The Sicilian economy continued to decline during this period, in part because the infamous bubonic plague, also known as the "black death," had by this time come to the island. The plague, at its height, would devastate most of fourteenth century Europe.

It was at this same time, because all sides in the almost century-old Sicilian war were now exhausted, that peace finally came to the island by default. In 1372, to get Naples to finally recognize Sicilian independence, Frederick IV had to agree, like his father before him, to call himself King of Trinacria and pay an annual tribute. The Papacy also agreed to peace, once Frederick accepted the traditional over-lordship of the Pope and agreed to help finance a papal war in northern Italy.

When Frederick IV died in 1377, his heir was his young daughter, Maria. Immediately, the question arose regarding her future, especially in terms of marriage. Whoever her husband would be, he would, through marriage, also have a claim on the Sicilian throne. Thus, many different political factions had an interest in any plans for the young heiress. The Pope wanted her, for example, to marry one of his nephews, while the the King of Aragon took this opportunity to renew his own claims on the island. And, the city-state of Milan and the kingdom of Naples also had an interest in Sicily. Meanwhile, however, the leading Sicilian baron, Artale D'Alagona, who was Maria's guardian, had other plans. He had decided to divide the island into four main spheres of influence. He himself would control the eastern part from his stronghold at Catania, The baron Guglielmo Peralta would govern the south from Sciacca, Manfredi Chiaramonte, would control the region around Palermo as well as the large holding of Modica in the south-east, and Francesco Ventimiglia, Count of Geraci, would administer the north coast. In fact, mutual jealousies among the barons, made this experiment short-lived. Finally, D'Alagona had hoped to gain an alliance for himself by marrying Maria to the ambitious Giangaleazzo Visconti, the ruler of Milan, but the Sicilian baron Raimondo Moncada, angered at his exclusion from the territorial division of the island, abducted Maria and took her to Barcelona. There, in 1390, she was married to the prince Martin, the grandson of the King of Aragon.

Martin and the Aragonese soon planned another conquest of Sicily. Of course, the Sicilian barons quickly realized that they might lose their new independence and the power they exerted over the island to this new king. They knew also that they would be replaced on their lands by a new group of foreign feudal nobles. So, they quickly convened a parliament at Castronovo. Conflicting rivalries of the baronial families, however, made agreement impossible. In fact, several major baronial families had already begun negotiating separately with the Aragonese. Martin, meanwhile, had raised an army by promising Sicilian lands to soldiers and nobles in Spain and even recruited criminals to join his invasion forces. Troops from other Spanish provinces also joined in.

In 1392, a Spanish force, under the general Bernardo Cabrera, invaded the island. Immediately, two of the major barons, or "vicars," of the four regions came over to Cabrera while the head of the Chiaramonte house, who had held Palermo against the invaders, was captured and executed. Then, Palermo fell to the Spanish and Chiaramonte's estates were given to Cabrera. The other chief cities quickly surrendered to the Spanish and Martin was soon in control of the rest of the island. He granted confiscated lands to his followers and set about restoring the royal prerogatives. The treaty of 1372 was annulled and Martin, now calling himself King of Sicily, repudiated the papal overlordship. He also claimed the title of the Apostolic Legateship, which gave him the right to appoint bishops and direct the Sicilian Church. But, Martin was able neither to totally dominate the Sicilian barons nor maintain a complete independence for his kingdom from Aragon.

Parliaments were convened and at these, Martin had to listen to the demands of his Sicilian subjects that he appoint fewer Catalans and more Sicilians to chief administrative posts on the island. Also, the request was made at these meetings that the Sicilian, rather than the Catalan law, be used in governing the island. Moreover, it was proposed that members of parliament be allowed to sit on the royal council and exercise some executive powers. This last proposal, in particular, was rejected by Martin who then instead proceeded to introduce Spanish law and procedures to the island. In reality, because Martin I remained under the influence of his father, the king of Aragon, Sicily became, at this time, almost a province of the Spanish realm. In fact, when he died, Martin bequeathed the kingdom of Sicily to his father as if it had been his personal property. With the king's subsequent death, Sicily came under the regency of Queen

Bianca of Aragon. A period of struggle among the baronial families for control of the island ensued.

The cities of Sicily themselves, although they wanted peace so as to be able continue their trade, were also divided. For a time, the Pope tried to veto the Aragonese claims and put forth the candidacy of Ladislas of Naples to be the new king of Sicily, but Palermo and other areas resisted. Finally, back in Spain, a new monarch was chosen for Sicily. Nine delegates from the Spanish kingdoms of Aragon, Catalonia, and Valencia elected as the island's ruler, Ferdinand, a member of a related branch of the dynasty of Castile. There was little resistance to this decision in Sicily itself. Generally, the people there seemed relieved that the divisions on the island would now come to an end and there would again be the possibility of a stable government.

But the new king, although he swore to uphold the island's traditional laws and prerogatives, had no intention of residing there. Sicily would no longer be the home of a king but instead, for the next four centuries, be administered by a viceroy. Of the 78 successive viceroys, however, very few would be Sicilian. The first sent to govern was Juan di Peñafiel, Ferninand's son. Actually, a faction in Messina had even, for a time, tried to make him king, but he refused and, after this, there would be few attempts to establish an independent monarchy.

After Ferdinand's death, Sicily's dependence on Spain was reinforced during the long reign of his son, Alfonso. Once he had taken Naples from the Angevins, Alfonso made that city, and not Palermo the permanent capital for both parts of the kingdom. Sicily would now be referred to as one of "two Sicilies," the Sicily "beyond the straits" as opposed to the Sicily "on this side of the straits," meaning the more important region of Naples. Although many of King Alfonso's policies were not productive for Sicily, especially in terms of trade—a war with Venice, for instance, caused the Venetians to burn the commercial fleet in Syracuse harbor—the Sicilian nobility supported him because he had tied his dynastic interests to those of the aristocratic classes. Barons could now hold territory that had originally been illegally acquired and could demand oaths of allegiance from, as well as tax, their own tenants. The barons were allowed also to maintain their own courts of justice in place of the royal courts. The family of Ventimiglia especially, was granted great privilege and authority over their tenants who then became the virtual subjects of their lords.

Because he was an enthusiastic and generous patron of the arts and of humanism, Alfonso was given the appellation of "the Magnanimous" and during his reign Sicily did emerge from the medieval period into the Renaissance. A school for Greek studies was set up in Messina and the first university in Sicily was founded at Catania. The latter was established to keep intellectual and scholars from emigrating to the mainland for their studies and research.

There was, however, also much corruption during Alfonso's reign. Because he was in constant need of revenues, he often imposed the *collecta,* a feudal tax that was supposed to be collected only in emergencies. Known later under its Spanish name of the *donativo,* this tax was now imposed as an annual grant payable to the king by the barons, the church, and the citizens of the cities. New offices, titles, and tax privileges were instituted merely as sources of revenue and no crime was ever considered so great that a pardon could not be purchased from the crown. And, although there is little evidence of great or widespread poverty or unemployment in Sicily during the early fifteenth century, economic conditions on the island continued to decline. Not much capital was being used for agricultural improvement, especially in the interior regions, and little money was spent on protecting the coastal trading regions from piracy. The tenants on the *latifundia* were still abused by their landlords and, in many areas, remained isolated from developments. In some parts of the interior, for instance, the peasants still spoke and dressed as their Arab ancestors did centuries before. The barons also took the best products of their tenant farmers and, through the policy of enclosure, began to shut out the shepherds who needed access to the common lands to graze their flocks. To all of these injustices, there was little redress. Even when they had the law on their side, few of the common people had the means and knowledge to bring their cases to the royal courts. In fact, the alternative system of local baronial justice was officially recognized by the crown.

Outside of the major cities there was not much of a commercial or professional middle class thus, during this period, the baronial class grew at the expense of the cities and their autonomy. In a sense, the cities preferred whatever peace and order direct royal control brought to the factionalism and rivarly that took place both within and between the island's major cities. Counter to earlier laws and traditions, some cities, now in debt, were sold into feudal servitude, in which case their powers of jurisdiction were purchased by a baron. This was the fate of many towns which then, to buy back their freedom, had to enter into a state of permanent debt. Syracuse,

Lentini, Sciacca, Corleone, and Cefalù, for example were all sold into servitude by Alfonso.

There were, of course, revolts and uprisings, practically in every town. But these usually were sparked by local grievances or the demand for immediate reforms and therefore tended to be short-lived. Internal rivalries, or rivalries between the cities, prevented the development of a common political interests among the towns-people. Meanwhile, cities such as Catania, Messina, and Palermo contended with each other for preeminence or to be the seat of residence of the viceroy or site of a parliament. It was, in fact, through the efforts of Catania and Messina that Palermo was never granted a university of its own, to the detriment of the whole island.

At this time, foreign merchants and bankers, especially the Spanish, began to gain influence and control in the Sicilian cities. They provided the king with what he needed at Naples, and in return received special privileges in Sicily. Mainland Italian merchants and bankers too, continued to play an important part in the development of the island, with many coming from Pisa, Florence, Genoa, and Venice to either settle in Sicilian cities or maintain consulates and trading centers there. There were many English merchants too, established mainly at Messina and Trapani where they were especially involved in the cloth and mineral trades. And, the Dalmatian city of Ragusa, today called Dubrovnik, also maintained a large colony of merchants in Sicily. These merchants historically had a protected and privileged status in Mediterranean trade, being both subjects of the Turkish Sultan and under the direct protection of the Pope. They also formed an important part of the economy at Messina.

In 1458, Alfonso died and Naples was given to an illegitimate son while his other kingdoms, including Sicily, were given to his brother John. The Sicilian subjects, of course, had no say in the matter. The Straits of Messina were again to become a barrier as the new King John, in 1459, separated Sicily even further from the rest of Italy. He proclaimed that from then on the island should never again be a kingdom separate from Aragon. Although John did not have a large number of soldiers in Sicily to help uphold his actions, there seems not to have been any real resistance from the people.

But, a Parliament did meet at Caltagirone, where the king had to listen to other political and economic grievances of his people, and at that time it was requested that, from then on, the eldest son of the King of Aragon should always be the viceroy of the island. This request was refused, but other concessions were granted, except if they conflicted with the direct interests of Spain. In return, Sicily remained loyal and even refused a request by Catalonia to assist in a rebellion against the king. The Sicilian parliament also voted to send a grant to help Aragon subdue the Moors of Granada, and large amounts of Sicilian gold were sent to Spain at this time.

The parliament, in fact, very rarely refused any government request for taxation, but in 1478 one of the few direct confrontations over such matters did occur. The viceroy wanted money for a war against the Turks and to put down a revolt in Sardinia. As he visited the towns to gain support for this request, however, he met with resistance. The Turkish war was seen as being fought only in the Spanish interest while, for Sicily, it was detrimental to trade. When the parliament finally met in Palermo, the citizens of that city prevented the representatives from voting for the new tax. In response, the viceroy moved the parliament to Catania, but to no avail. The tax was never granted and the viceroy was replaced.

In 1479, King John was succeeded by his son Ferdinand who, with his wife Isabella, would unite the Spanish kingdoms of Aragon and Castile. The Iberian peninsula was becoming a single nation and, in the context of this new Spanish empire, Sicily was destined to take on a smaller and less significant role. Even though taxes were increased, local interests were now generally disregarded. At the same time, the Spanish wars continued to be financial burdens for the Sicilian people. In 1495, because Ferdinand decided to take southern Italy from his cousin, Sicily had to once more support an expensive military enterprise. In 1504, Naples was conquered, making it a Spanish possession. This meant that again there would be two "Sicilies"—the island and the southern mainland—both sharing the same government at Naples. It was also at this time that Sicily had to accept the introduction of the Spanish Inquisition. Its headquarters on the island would be at Palermo but orders were given from Spain. The Inquisition had originally been established in the thirteenth century by the Catholic Church for the purpose of detecting, examining, and punishing heretics. It spread throughout Europe, but became especially powerful in Spain and in the Spanish territories.

In the period from 1510 to 1525, a number of insurrections did take place on the island, but these seemed to be more uprisings by the feudal barons than popular rebellions against the Spanish rule. One rebellion, however, that occurred in 1516, against the policies of the viceroy Moncada, did have the characteristics of a popular uprising. Moncada been sent to prepare Sicily as military base for a conquest of North Africa. Needing large sums of money, he abruptly disregarded local tradition and custom and confiscated whatever he thought necessary for his military expenses. He also tried to suspend the popular St. Cristina's fair at Palermo, during which local merchants were excused from excise taxes and duties. The people were outraged and violence erupted. Finally, Moncada punished some citizens after a mob riot had broken out over the actions of soldiers who, returning from North Africa unpaid, had begun to confiscate food supplies. A general feeling of resistance to his rule was clearly evident.

Upon news of the king's death back in Spain that year, the Sicilian parliament declared that the viceroy's authority had come to an end. Moncada, in response, dissolved parliament, but that body simply reassembled at Termini. Meanwhile, a popular revolution broke out in Palermo. The Spanish administrators in the city were attacked and rioting broke out everywhere. For almost a year, the government there was in abeyance. But, the nobility proclaimed their own loyalty to the Spanish king and the city of Messina, too, showed support for the viceroy. Finally, as a compromise, Moncada suggested to the king that he appoint an Italian viceroy. In 1517, a Neapolitan, the Count of Montelone, took over the government. However, while he instituted some reforms, this new viceroy provoked the baronial class into a rebellion by questioning some of their traditional privileges.

As a result, another revolt soon broke out, this one led by a nobleman, Squarcialupo, who had also been a leader in the Palermo uprising. Squarcialupo succeeded in taking over the city and, until he was assassinated, ruled for a short time as a popular dictator. A third revolt, in 1523, led by members of the Imperatore family and backed by France, was also quickly suppressed by the Spanish government, this time with more severity. The brothers Imperatore were executed and their bodies left in cages as a warning to others.

By now, there was a new king back in Spain and a new dynasty. Ferdinand, who died in 1516, left no male heirs. His empire was inherited by his grandson, Charles V, of the Austrian House of Hapsburg. As Charles's vast empire included all of Spain, other large European and Mediterranean holdings, and the vast overseas colonial territories that were claimed by the Spanish crown, Sicily was drawn even more into the orbit of that empire. Consequently, the island would now be considered even less a part of Italy and, for the next three centuries, Spanish politics would dominate Sicilian affairs.

X

Spanish Rule in Sicily

THE LONG PERIOD OF SPANISH RULE HAS SOMETIMES BEEN BLAMED FOR the corruption of Sicily, especially in terms of the island's economic decline and its related social problems. Certainly, as Spanish kings did rule the island for more than four centuries, that nation's influence was considerable. But the actual nature, extent, and real effect of that influence is difficult to measure. How much was the attitude of *spagnolismo* due to Spanish rule itself?

The policy of the Spanish viceroys was, of course, one of conserving the status quo. And, as these administrators were not specifically charged with instituting reforms, major innovations or improvements were not their primary goals. They were merely supposed to hear the complaints of the people, make periodic tours of the island, and keep law and order. As their reports indicate, the viceroys did not themselves attempt to initiate any new methods or policies. Each simply followed the pattern of his predecessor.

The position of viceroy itself was a most coveted post, and most chosen for that position were from the grandée class of the Spanish nobility. In Madrid there was a State Council for Italy that governed affairs for the Spanish territories there, but although one Sicilian usually sat on the Council, the majority of its members were Spaniards. The system did, however, incorporate some checks and balances. The viceroy's deputy at Palermo (called the *consultor*) even had, for example, some independent powers. There were also *visitadors,* or investigators, sent from Spain every twenty years to report on the administration of the island. Meanwhile, while revolts against the Spanish rule did sometimes occur, the population generally had become resigned to a foreign government. The people had, of course, experienced foreign governments before and knew therefore that they did bring certain benefits and security. Also, in a sense, a sectionalism too had developed, in which the Sicilians gave their primary loyalty to their city or town. Messina and Palermo, for instance, were great rivals, so that if one rose against the Spanish government the other would, in contrast, support it. Moreover, the Spanish administration helped the upper classes in the cities maintain their various privileges.

From the sixteenth century on, any interest that the King of Spain had in Sicily mostly concerned the help that the island could give towards the strengthening of his own dynastic power in Europe and the Mediterranean. Militarily, Sicily was important to the Spanish Empire in its war with the Ottoman Turks. From the island, bases could be established in North Africa and other Mediterranean areas to fight both the Turks and the Barbary pirates who were hindering trade. Sicily itself was vulnerable to pirate attacks, especially the coastal areas, and the harbors at Palermo, Messina, and Augusta all had to be fortified. For this security, the population, it seems, gave their money in taxes with little complaint, but at least one viceroy found that the Sicilians themselves were not interested in joining the mercenary forces that were traditionally employed for war at this time. "It is not their nature to be warlike," the viceroy noted in a report to Madrid.

Between the Sicilian nobility and the Spanish crown there was usually cooperation, as they had certain basic common interests. The kings of Spain continued to maintain the royal prerogatives of former rulers, but Sicily would never experience again the strong monarchies of the past. The days of Roger and Frederick II were gone. What both the King of Spain and the Sicilian nobility wanted was peace and order with a minimum of Spanish troops kept on the island.

Under the Spanish monarchs, the number of noble titles greatly increased. In 1500, there were seven counts; by 1600, twenty one families held that rank. The first Sicilian dukedom was created in 1556 for the di Luna family of Sciacca. And, by the end of the 16th century, there were four princes among the ranks of the nobility. Princedoms, in fact, multiplied rapidly so that by the next century one hundred and two princely titles had been granted. This was in a population of about one million. With these noble titles came expenses. The nobles each had to maintain a large retinue of servants and lavish liveries and coaches. A palace, especially at Palermo near the viceroy's residence, was always a goal of these new noble houses. Much was spent on the buying of titles and privileges and the nobility had little time to pay attention to the needs of the Sicilian economy or to improvements for the island.

Spanish rule actually both helped and hindered the expansion of the economy of Sicily. Some reports of the 16th century go as far as to describe the island as the richest of Spain's possessions but, in fact, the revenues were only half that of Naples or Milan. The true wealth of Sicily was, as it had always been, in its agriculture. Inasmuch as this was a productive time, the island experienced a short "St. Martin's Summer" (or "Indian Summer" as it is also known) of relative prosperity. It was in the period from 1501 to 1590 that the population of the island, excluding Palermo and Messina, rose from approximately a half million to over eight hundred thousand and the export prices of grain, the main resource, remained at a steady level. But, the favorable conditions that made all of this possible lasted only for a short period. At this time, also, the climate of the island seems to have become dryer and more arid than it had been in the earlier Arab and Norman periods. As a result of this, there was, beginning in 1575, three consecutive years of famine. Then, at the end of the 16th century, Sicily had more or less ceased to be a big grain exporter. This was due, in part, to a population increase, but also because competition from producers in northern Italy and in the East had increased. Another factor was probably an impoverishment and subsequent exhaustion of the soil.

In 1669, there would be a large eruption of Mount Etna. There had been minor eruptions of Mount Etna before but that of 1669 was the worst of all. A river of lava a mile wide flowed for over fifteen miles, crushing the walls of Catania and filling up part of the port. Whole areas of the countryside were devastated. Later, in 1693, a great earthquake did even more damage, almost totally destroying Noto and Modica, and leaving Syracuse, Catania, and Ragusa in ruins. Perhaps five percent of the island's population died as a result of the quake and the subsequent spread of infection and disease. Whole areas of the society came to a halt and Sicily's only university was completely destroyed. One result of this disaster was that large sections of the city of Catania were rebuilt with dark lava stone that was used to construct new and beautiful Baroque palaces and churches. Today, there even can be seen, in the main square of that city, the Piazza del Duomo, an elephant carved from lava, bearing a granite Egyptian obelisk on its back. It is now the symbol of Catania. The nearby town of Noto, which was largely destroyed, was also rebuilt, but on a different site than the original one. That is why Noto is a completely Baroque city today. Unlike other Sicilian cities, which reflect varied and overlapping architectural styles, Noto is the expression of only one single period and style. It is really a unique and magnificent example of the Baroque Age. The most outstanding figure of Sicilian culture in the 17th century, the historian Rocco Pirri, was from Noto, as were the great 15th century humanists, Giovanni Aursipa and Antonio Cassarino. In terms of the cultural developments of this period, it is appropriate to mention too, the work of the 16th century Sicilian painter, Pietro Novelli, known as "il Monrealese." As his name implies, he was from Monreale and, by the time of his death in 1634, he had earned the reputation of being one of the greater painters of the period, his work rivaling that of Van Dyck and Caravaggio.

In summary, a large part of the history of Spanish rule in Sicily in the first half of the seventeenth century is a story above all of heavy duties, special contributions and grants and, in a word, of taxation. It is in this sense then that it is also a history of revolt. But these revolts, unlike others in Europe during this period, were mostly confined to the towns. The first such occurred in Palermo in 1647 over conditions caused by a famine. But it was shortly suppressed through the efforts of both the barons and the viceroy. The second uprising was at Messina in 1674, and it had its origin in the traditional rivalry of this city with Palermo. It was this revolt which gave the French a pretext for intervening in the affairs of the island.

At the end of the 17th century, the rule of the Spanish Hapsburg dynasty came to an end. The King, Charles II, had died without a male heir and so the crown passed, through French influence, to Charles's French Bourbon grandson. This did not please the other European powers and so the War of the Spanish Succession would be fought to contest the arrangement. Sicily played a key role in that conflict. The Austrians wanted to put the Hapsburg Archduke Charles on the Spanish throne to prevent both a possible union of France and Spain, and to stop Sicily from becoming a base for French expansion in the Mediterranean. Under the new Spanish King, the Bourbon Philip V, who began a new dynasty, French influence could already be seen on the island. Messina, which had been a French ally, was restored to its former position and large holdings of the Spanish nobility in Sicily who had backed the Austrian claimant, ·were confiscated. In 1707, there was a revolt in Palermo against the new rulers, sparked by the billeting of Irish and French mercenaries in the citizens' homes. Finally, the viceroy was persuaded to send these mercenaries to Messina.

The war continued, and there were small invasions and landings by foreign forces including those of the English, who had also joined the conflict. But, before any large scale invasion or revolt could take place, a meeting of the major European powers at Utrecht was held to find a solution to the conflict. It was decided to take Sicily from the Spanish Bourbon King Philip V and give it to his father-in-law, Duke Victor Amadeus of Savoy. Thus, in 1713, the long period of Spanish rule in Sicily abruptly came to an end. The 18th century was now to see several different dynasties contest control of the kingdom while, in time, the new and dynamic revolutionary ideas of the age would help to bring about important political and social reforms.

XI
The 18th Century

THE TRANSITION IN SICILY TO THE RULE OF THE HOUSE OF SAVOY IN 1713 was challenged by the Austrian House of Hapsburg which, at this time, controlled Naples. However, England, preferring to see a smaller power installed in the island, backed the Duke of Savoy of Piedmont's claims to sovreignty. The English were especially interested in maintaining free trade in the Mediterranean and in keeping Sicily, which of course also had strategic importance, out of the hands of another major power. Thus, it came to be that in the first half of the 18th century the Sicilian people would be ruled by four different dynasties. After 13 years under the Spanish Bourbons, Sicily for five years came under the control of the House of Savoy. This would be followed by 14 years under Austrian Hapsburgs, who were then succeeded by the Neapolitan Bourbons.

When King Victor Amadeus of Savoy arrived by English ship at Palermo in 1713 he was the first monarch to have visited the island since 1535. He remained for a year and, during that time, visited the main coastal cities, trying to understand the problems of the area. Some improvements were made, the University of Catania, for example, was reestablished, and efforts were undertaken to improve the economy. Then, after a year, he left. But his administrators inherited many of the problems of their Spanish predecessors and, although there were no revolts, the regime really received little support. One beautiful and lasting result of Victor Amadeus's reign in Sicily, however, can be found back in his capital of Turin in Piedmont. During his brief period as King of Sicily, Victor Amadeus had the opportunity to summon to Turin one of the century's most brilliant architects, the Sicilian Filippo Juvarra, of Messina. Juvarra's masterpiece was the Superga Basilica, built between 1716 and 1731, on a hill overlooking Turin. It was erected to commemorate a victory of the Piedmontese forces in 1706, and is considered to be Juvarra's finest ecclesiastical structure.

In 1718, the Spanish navy arrived to reassert Spain's claim to Sicily. King Victor Amadeus asked for Austrian help and, as a result, the War of the Quadruple Alliance began. Victor Amadeus had already promised Austria the island in exchange for Sardinia, so long as he could continue to call himself a King.

The Austrian and Spanish armies met in Sicily and, at the huge battle at Francavilla—the largest military engagement on the island since Roman times—the Austrians were victorious. Victor Amadeus of Savoy became the King of Sardinia and the Austrian Hapsburg Emperor Charles became the King of Sicily by conquest.

For 14 years, the Austrian administration attempted to make the rule of Sicily a profitable venture for the Hapsburg dynasty. But, like the Savoy government before it, this administration lacked the patience and determination, as well as an understanding of the island and its people that were needed to make the endeavor successful. One reason for this is that the people and the local barons had, during the years of Spanish rule, become accustomed to a more distant, and in some ways, more easy going government, and resented the attempts by these new powers to institute rapid and unsettling changes.

In 1734, when international tensions tended to isolate Austria, the Spanish took advantage of the situation and launched an expedition to retake the island. While there had been no Sicilian rebellion against the Austrians, the people in general welcomed the Spanish and, as the Austrian army did not put up much of a fight, the invading forces quickly took control. The Sicilians suddenly found their land again joined to the Kingdom at Naples under Spanish control. The new ruler would be a son of the Spanish King, to be known as Charles III.

Under the preceding regimes, the long established Spanish influence never really disappeared. The nobility, especially, followed Spanish traditions and etiquette, despite the efforts of the Austrians to introduce the social customs of Vienna. At the same time, the definite undercurrent of Italian culture on the island became stronger. Many of the viceroys had been Italians and use of the Italian language was becoming increasingly common, side by side with the Sicilian dialect. In 1741, Parliament was opened for the first time with a speech read by the viceroy in Italian.

In 1759, when King Charles was named to the throne of Spain, the rest of the European powers did not want him to retain the titles of Sicily and Naples. As a compromise, those two kingdoms were given to his eight-year old son who would be known in Sicily as

Ferdinand III. It was during his long reign of 66 years that Sicily would strongly develop the ties binding her to Italy. Ferdinand's dynasty, known as the Neapolitan Bourbons, at first hoped that they would succeed where the Austrians and Piedmontese had failed. But instead of welcoming these changes, the Sicilian Parliament asked the King to restore things to the way they were.

The Sicilian Parliament traditionally traced its origins back to Roman times. Although this was titious, there was still a great romantic history attached to that institution. Its three houses, or *bracci,* were proudly cited as the champions of liberty against foreign rule and the openings and closings of the Parliament were celebrated with great ceremony. The three Houses represented the upper clergy, the nobles, and the townsmen.

In commercial terms, the life of the island was determined by the prevailing economic system of the age: mercantilism. In the mercantile system, the major powers, Spain, France, and Britain, maintained territories and colonies for the economic benefit of the mother country. Exports were favored totally over imports, and the colonies were expected to buy only the products of the ruling nation. For Sicily, this meant that Spanish goods had to be taken in trade almost exclusively. In such a system, smuggling flourished. Just as in the British colonies in North America, illicit cargoes were smuggled in, and there were even episodes in Sicilian ports similar to the Boston Tea Party, in which enforced items were thrown overboard from ships in protest of mercantile duties and quotas.

But the 18th century was also the time of the Enlightenment, the Age of Reason. Throughout Europe, intellectuals emerged such as Voltaire, Rousseau, Smith, Beccaria, and others, who criticized and reexamined existing political, social, and economic institutions. While these thinkers differed in their interpretations and recommendations for the improvement of society, what they had in common was both a faith in reason as the guiding principle in all matters and an optimistic view that the social and political order could be improved. Their influence helped to inspire both the American and French Revolutions. In Sicily too, the works of these thinkers, or *philosophes* as they were called, were being read and applied to such local issues as the latifundia system as well as other institutions which were considered outmoded or unjust. In fact, the thinkers of the Englightenment were really concerned with all aspects of learning, that is the natural as well as the social sciences, and it is in the former that there emerged, from amongst the Sicilian aristocracy, individuals who would contribute to that field of knowledge. The Baron of

San Giaime e Pozzo, for instance, in 1735 produced a manual of agriculture, while at the same time Prince Biscari at Catania, who had a reputation of benevolency and a progressive policy towards his servants and workers, built up one of the finest private museums in the world. And, Filippo Arena, who is considered a founder of modern biology and Giuseppe Balsamo, known also as Cagliostro, were both born in Sicily in the 18th century. Cagliostro has been called the greatest adventurer of all times and is credited with having predicted to King Louis XVI of France the coming French Revolution. Unfortunately, he was not believed. Meanwhile, the writings of the other major figures of the Enlightenment circulated among the Sicilian aristocracy, continuing to exert an influence.

It was under this influence and quest for knowledge that a new academy was founded at Palermo. Twenty endowed chairs were established at the school and and a surgical theater was also built. Telescopes for the academy were purchased in London and Paris for the astronomy classes, and equipment was installed for the teaching of physics. Students were even sent abroad to study agriculture and veterinary science. At the same time, technical schools were opened for poorer children in which weaving, glass-making, and ceramics were taught. And, three state schools were set up for the children of the nobility. One of these was described by an English visitor as "far superior to Eton." These changes in Sicily during the eighteenth century became possible because certain individuals were now convinced that modifications and improvements in education, law, economics, and politics would all be advantageous to the island's development.

But, more effective than the efforts of individual reformers was the fact that Sicily had now become directly exposed to the main currents of European thought. A factor contributing to this contact was the development of what might be called an early type of tourism. The island was gaining a reputation as a most picturesque and romantic site to visit, but it was an early travel volume, published in 1773 by Patrick Brydone, that really popularized Sicily as a tourist spot. Many other authors followed with similar works, all of which attested to the island's diversity, quaintness, and its abundance of historic locations. With its volcanoes, folklore, and remains of classical antiquity, there was something in Sicily for everyone. In the final analysis, however, no one helped to popularize and romanticize the island's splendor and beauty more than the great figure of the age, the German Romantic poet and novelist, J. W. Goethe. Goethe's moving and poetic descriptions of the natural beauty of Sicily, combined with the art and architecture left by the ages, was what first enticed many travelers to journey south to see for themselves the sights that had so much inspired the poet. In 1787, for instance, describing the beauty of the panorama at Taomina, he wrote that it was "where art has come to the aid of nature." In the following passage, on the view from the Greek theater there, Goethe perhaps best recounts the charm of the island:

> Whoever goes to the highest point, where once the audience gathered, cannot do less than admit that people at an ordinary theatre have, perhaps, never seen a sight like this one. To the right, above tall cliffs, rise some fortification; below, down there, the city. The view takes in the whole mountainous backbone of Etna, to the left the beach as far as Catania, nay as far as Syracuse. The enormous smoking volcano completes the immense picture . . . We could not drag ourselves away from this place before sunset. To watch this wonderful region, with all its interesting details, giving way little by little to darkness, is an unspeakably beautiful sight.

Many who followed, among them painters and other writers, were drawn by such descriptions, found in Goethe's *Travels in Italy* and, like him, were moved to tears when they first experienced the extraordinary beauty of the island.

These foreign visitors who came to Sicily helped, in turn, to bring the island and its people closer to developments occurring in Europe. Now, even more translations of the major works of the period were appearing in Sicilian bookstores and in private libraries. The works of such authors as Arthur Young, Hume, Locke, and Pope, as well as those of Diderot, Voltaire, Rousseau, and the other philosophes were now becoming familiar to the educated classes.

This period also saw a rise in the status of Palermo as a center of public and cultural life. It was then the largest city in Italy except for Naples and, because of the series of disasters and plagues had just struck Messina, Palermo, for the moment, eclipsed that city in its relationship to the rest of the island. A major event in the life of Palermo was the festival of St. Rosalia, which is still celebrated today. Held in July, after the wheat harvest, the festival lasts for almost a week and during that time, which is preceded by weeks of preparation, all work comes to a halt. Each successive mayor of the city tried to outdo his predecessor in organizing memorable celebrations for the feast, whose highlight was a huge fireworks display. Traditionally, the many crafts guilds too played a role in the celebrations.

But in the 18th century, Palermo was also the scene of a popular uprising that was brought about by a bad harvest and a general discontent among the lower classes. In 1773, when food supplies ran short, riots broke out. It was only with great effort that the viceroy and the Spanish authorities restored order. To the administration, it was clear that reforms had to be instituted. In fact, these soon were to be implemented.

From 1781 until 1786, Sicily was under the administration of the viceroy Caracciolo, who would be responsible for a program of reform more sweeping than any since the thirteenth century. Caracciolo first began his program of reform by suppressing the Inquisition on the island. That institution once held great power, even over the viceroy, but by the eighteenth century was considered an outdated relic of a bygone era.

Next, Caracciolo targeted several of the privileges of the nobility. In his opinion, privilege was deserved only if there was corresponding public service and leadership. The aristocrats were to be the leaders and caretakers of society and not just the recipients of its benefits. Many archaic feudal privileges were abolished and the basis for the latifundia system was also questioned. Of course, there was opposition from the landed barons, but Caracciolo tried, unsuccessfully, to persuade the King to visit the island to show the people that there was a higher authority than the baronial class.

Although in time Caracciolo was, through the demands of the barons, eventually recalled, his successor, the Prince of Caramanico, was determined to carry on his predecessor's policies. Taxation reform was achieved and the feudal system was further diminished. The enlightened spirit of the eighteenth century, which had inspired these policies, had taken root on the island and would soon help to bring Sicily into the age of revolution. The catalyst was the French Revolution of 1789.

When the revolution broke out in France in 1789, it was indeed seen by many as the beginning of a new age for mankind. By the end of the century, as Napoleon with his armies spread the enthusiasm and ideals of that revolution throughout Europe, Sicily too would receive the spirit of this new age. But revolution also brings war, and as the conflict developed between France and the other major European powers, Sicily would take on a special importance as a strategic base in the Mediterranean for Napoleon's chief opponent, the British. With that, a new chapter would also begin in the island's history.

Animated Clock Tower, Messina. Among the many figures depicted on the famous animated clock tower of Messina, are those of Dina and Clarentia, the heroines who warned the city of a French attack during the Sicilian Vespers uprising of 1282.

The Fountain of the Elephant, Catania. This symbol of the city of Catania features a large elephant carved from lava from the 1669 eruption of Mt. Etna, supporting a granite Egyptian obelisk that once stood in a nearby Roman arena. Under the rule of Aragon, Catania once again became a prosperous and flourishing city. (Courtesy of the Italian Cultural Institute of New York.)

Baroque Church of San Giuseppe, Ragusa. During the long period of Spanish rule in Sicily, the baroque style of architecture flourished. Many outstanding examples of that style, such as this church in Ragusa, were erected during the rebuilding that took place in several Sicilian cities after the great earthquake of 1693. (Courtesy of the Italian Cultural Institute of New York.)

View of Taormina. During the Eighteenth Century, Sicily first became a favorite tourist spot, especially for travelers from the North
of Europe. The German poet Goethe, in his description of the
beautiful panorama at Taormina wrote that is was "where art has
come to the aid of nature." He also described Sicily as the "key to all
of Italy." (Courtesy of the Italian Cultural Institute of New York.)

The Bourbon Chinese Villa, Palermo. Reflecting the period's taste for the exotic, this Chinese Villa was built in 1799 to serve as a residence for Sicily's Bourbon rulers during their exile from Naples. Standing in La Favorita Park, it is now a museum. The Bourbons were to be Sicily's last rulers before the island became a part of united Italy. (Courtesy of the Italian Cultural Institute of New York.)

Giuseppe Garibaldi. The hero of Italian unification, Giuseppe Garibaldi, landed in Sicily in 1860 with his "Thousand Red Shirts" to begin the liberation of the island and its incorporation into the new united Kingdom of Italy. He is seen here on his island home of Caprera.

Barricades at Porta Macqueda. Barricades such as these were used at Palermo during Garibaldi's decisive battle in his campaign to liberate Sicily in 1860. His victory was achieved with the help of his "Thousand Red Shirts" and the efforts of the brave Sicilian volunteers who had joined his forces.

King Victor Emmanuel II. Victor Emmanuel II (1820–1878) in 1861 became the first ruler of a united Italy and Sicily's first Italian monarch.

XII
The Age of Revolution

BY 1798, THE REVOLUTIONARY FRENCH ARMIES, LED BY NAPOLEON Bonaparte, had advanced beyond the borders of their nation to conquer other territories. Soon, they had control of the Italian peninsula. At Naples, the Bourbon ruler, Ferdinand, with most of his court and under the protection of the British, had fled the advancing French forces. They arrived in Sicily and reestablished the royal court at Palermo. The island was free from French control. Napoleon himself, of course, had intended to also invade Sicily, but when his troops were finally ready to cross over from Calabria they found that their own navy had failed to provide enough ships for the crossing. (Later in 1808, when the French finally had a second opportunity to invade, Napoleon, distracted by events in the eastern Mediterranean, instead ordered his forces to occupy Corfu and the Greek islands).

The arrival of Ferdinand in Sicily in 1800 would be that king's first visit to his Sicilian domains in over forty years. The people there generally supported their monarch against the French and, for many, there was even the hope that he would proclaim Sicily an independent kingdom in its own right, under the Bourbons but separate from Naples. These hopes were encouraged by the fact that, as soon as the king and his retinue arrived, Palermo once more became the site of a royal court. Soon, however, it was clear that, although the island did benefit in terms of prestige due to the royal presence, the cost of supporting the monarchy now fell completely on the Sicilian people. The king, his court, and the hundreds of Neapolitan officials who fled with him, had to be sustained solely out of the island's revenues, Naples being, at this point, completely under French control. Also, Ferdinand lavishly rewarded his British protectors with Sicilian lands and monies. Admiral Nelson, for example, on whose flagship the royal family escaped, was given a huge estate in Sicily and granted the title of Duke of Bronté.

By 1802, Ferdinand had set up his government and, in that year, personally presided over the opening of the Sicilian Parliament, the first monarch to do so since 1714. At that time, he promised that if he ever returned to Naples a second royal court would also be kept at Palermo. Soon, however he was to break this promise after a treaty with Napoleon allowed him to return to Naples, taking with him a large part of the Sicilian treasury. When war started again in 1806, and the royal family had to once more flee to Palermo, they received a much cooler reception from their Sicilian subjects. Ferdinand, however, remained unconcerned, and actually, it was his strong-willed wife, Maria Carolina (a sister of the ill-fated queen, Marie Antoinette of France) who really ran the government. Ferdinand, instead, spent most of his time in hunting and other diversions and planning new residences to be built for the royal family. Among the luxuries the Bourbons built for themselves at this time is the park and game preserve at Palermo known as *La Favorita*. It features a beautiful residence, the *Palazzino Cinese,* constructed as a royal retreat. Its name derives from its Chinese design and motifs, a style popular with Europeans of the period. It is now a museum.

The Bourbons were, of course, concerned with the defense of the island, but, as there was no separate Sicilian army or navy, Ferdinand was forced to invite the British to take over that responsibility. The French always hoped to take Sicily and make it a base for their Mediterranean operations. Directly across the Straits of Messina, Napoleon's brother Joseph, who had been made King of the Two Sicilies after the French invasion, had massed thousands of French troops, all poised to invade. Only the presence of the British deterred them.

The British quickly made Sicily their own base and, with this large foreign force now stationed there, the island would experience a new prosperity. There was a direct subsidy sent by the British government, large loans, and private investments from London. The British troops themselves spent large amounts of money that also helped to stimulate the Sicilian economy. By 1812, there would be thirty British consulates established in various parts of the island. The population itself was never conscripted into the war, and the British presence also helped to deter the piracy that for so long had hindered Sicilian commerce. Eventually, there would be over 17,000 British troops in Sicily and Britain would finally take over most of the costs of government.

There was, however, some dissatisfaction with the British presence, especially among the baronial class. To supplement the costs of government, Ferdinand had begun to ask for a suspension of the barons' tax immunities. This constituted a major break with tradition because, for centuries, the baronial class had been exempt from taxation. Now, with wartime inflation, the government had to ask for a suspension of that ancient privilege. The king had already such revenue-raising measures as non-parliamentary taxation, sales taxes, and the nationalization of certain properties. But the barons, through parliament, refused to cooperate any further. They even attempted rebellion but, as it amounted only to a half-hearted effort on the part of just a few of the nobility, the uprising was quickly suppressed. At this point, the king's ministers turned to the British for help. They asked the British commander, General William Bentinck, to take control of the government and institute a program of reform.

General Bentinck immediately began to set up a system of liberal parliamentary government for Sicily. He sought a compromise with the rebellious faction among the nobles and even appointed some of them to cabinet posts. Taxation reforms were instituted. A constitution was planned and parliament was to be restructured. Equality before the law became a right of every subject and freedom of the press was established for the first time. And, most revolutionary of all, feudalism was abolished. Surprisingly, both the monarchy and the conservative feudal lords at first accepted radical changes without a fight. The result of all of this was, that in 1812, the "ancien regimé," or old Bourbon order, had essentially come to an end.

But, in time, both the Bourbons and the landed Sicilian aristocracy grew unhappy over their loss of power. By 1814, royal agents were attempting to build up a party among the nobles and gain popular support among the urban poor and the guilds. Ferdinand was now determined to centralize the government and allow Sicily even less autonomy than it had known previously. Then, in 1815, after Napoleon's defeat by the British, Austrians, and other allied powers, the British began to withdraw from the island. Preoccupied with events elsewhere in Europe, they had conceded the Austrian influence in southern Italian affairs.

In 1816, with the approval of the Austrians, Ferdinand proclaimed himself Ferdinand I of a new unitary state, the Kingdom of the Two Sicilies. Previously, he had been known as Ferdinand IV of Naples and Ferdinand III of Sicily, because the two areas were considered, at least in theory, separate realms. This subtle change in title represented an important move to centralize the royal authority that would tie Sicily even closer to the mainland. It ended for all time the idea that the island constituted a separate kingdom. Now, under

Ferdinand's new regime, the Sicilian flag was abolished, as was also freedom of the press, and the king made it clear that he had no intention of ever again calling parliament. Actually, throughout all of Europe, this was a time of restoration and reaction, and Ferdinand was acting accordingly. All over the continent restored governments were attempting to suppress the ideas of liberty popularized by the French Revolution and replace them with the principles of the old order.

Soon, however, in Sicily, the rule from Naples became even more despised than that of any previous regime. Finally, in 1820, there was a popular rising in Palermo against what was to be perceived as an oppressive administration. That year, during the city's St. Rosalia festivities, the "tricolor," the new flag symbolizing Italian unity, appeared for the first time. It had always been forbidden by the Bourbon government. Throughout Palermo, there were demands for independence as the rebellion quickly spread to all neighborhoods and districts. Although eventually suppressed, this uprising was to be a prelude to the other nationalist revolts that were to follow, not only in Sicily, but throughout all of Italy.

Ferdinand died in 1825. He had been king for sixty-six years. Although this period ended in reaction, however, it should be remembered that during the earlier part of his reign, some reforms, especially in education, had been instituted. Also, in that period, certain improvements in the areas of health and medicine, notably vaccination, came to the kingdom. Ferdinand was succeeded by his frivolous and corrupt son, Francis I. But he ruled for only five years. Narrow minded and intolerant, Francis, during his brief reign, did little to improve the image of Bourbon rule in either Sicily or Naples.

In 1830, Francis was succeeded by his son, known as Ferdinand II. This new king had been born in Sicily and began his reign by making an effort at reform. During the early years of his rule, Ferdinand II would visit the island more than any monarch before him, encouraging there improvements in agriculture and industry. Also, at this time, in the field of education, scientific studies were encouraged, and Sicilians were given preference in the government posts on the island. But, in a real sense, these reforms came too late. The Sicilian people had never really been reconciled to the fact that their homeland had been made a Neapolitan possession and, by the 1830's, the ideas of revolution, that had already taken root elsewhere in Europe had, in Sicily, now fostered a new spirit of nationalism and independence.

But, besides being a most dynamic age in terms of political and national developments, the first half of the nineteenth century was also a time of dramatic development in industry and commerce. It was the period of the Industrial Revolution, and events would occur that were to change forever the face of modern society. These changes would be felt in Sicily, too.

The Industrial Revolution greatly transformed the areas of production, transportation, and communications. Already, during the British occupation of the island, such changes had already occurred, as for instance, in the operation of the Sicilian merchant marine. Because of technological improvements, Sicilian ships could now making frequent transatlantic runs. Soon, steam power was introduced, and the first Sicilian steam ship, the *Palermo,* was launched. In the same period, another major effect of the Industrial Revolution on the Sicilian economy was seen in the textile industry. Due to improvements in agriculture and weaving, both silk and cotton production increased, with more cotton eventually being grown in Sicily than anywhere else in Italy. And, the mining industry too, grew, as large amounts of foreign investment, especially French, came to the island stimulating growth in that area.

Because of the investment of British and French capital in the island, 440 miles of roadway, between 1839 and 1852, were added to the existing routes that had been opened by the Bourbon government. Between 1852 and 1860, 200 more miles were added. But these roads, however, were often no more than country lanes and, in winter, they would become swamps while in summer they were extremely dusty. It was for such conditions that the picturesque Sicilian carts were first built. In time, these colorful, two-wheeled, mule carts would become a symbol of the island. Painted with biblical scenes or themes from Sicilian history and folklore, they have been called "the world's most decorated vehicles."

The Industrial Revolution also was the age of the inventor and the entrepreneur. In Sicily, such "captains of industry" as Vincenzo Florio appeared, introducing important innovations in both commerce and industry. Florio, for example, helped to develop the banking industry at Palermo and, in 1841, also opened the Oretea machine shop and foundry, the first of its kind on the island. He even took part in the development of the Marsala wine industry, which had its start in the late 1700's when two British merchants William and John Woodhouse, came to Sicily to purchase raw materials for the making of soda. Arriving at Marsala, they tasted the local wine and found it remarkably similar to Portuguese and Spanish wines, such as Port, Madeira, and sherry, which were then quite popular in England. The

Woodhouses purchased several barrels of Marsala wine and sent them back to England where they met with immediate success. A flourishing trade soon began. One of the first customers who helped to popularize the wine was Lord Nelson. Marsala wine soon became a standard stable even for the rations of the British fleet—even now, the British navy still keeps a stock on board its ships. Today three of the most famous Marsala wineries, the companies of Florio, Woodhouse, and Ingram, founded during this period, are still in existence. These wineries can be visited and samples of their products tasted by the public.

In fact, despite industrial developments, Sicily's wealth has really always been in agriculture, and the majority of people in the nineteenth century continued to work on the land. Farming remained, as it had always been, the basis of the Sicilian economy. It was in this context, that during the first half of that century, the Sicilian wine industry expanded, while the growing of fruits, especially the citrus variety, also caused important advances in the agricultural sector. Olive oil production, in particular, increased with that product becoming a major export item. Moreover, important new crops, such as potatoes, were introduced, which helped to feed the growing population.

But, there were also drawbacks to the economic growth and development on the island during this period. For instance, as more individuals acquired status and property, a social attitude developed which looked down upon manual labor and instead encouraged acquisition of rank and title. Accumulated wealth was less admired than the acquisition of respect gained by being a *galantuomo*—one who did not have to work with his hands for a living. Thus, because official positions always carried with them a mark of social esteem, even small government positions were considered by many to be preferable to being a successful merchant or farmer. Nevertheless, economic improvements in Sicily did continue and such advancements were noticed by many important visitors to the island at this time. Among these, was the famous French writer and social thinker, Alexis de Tocqueville. Tocqueville was a frequently quoted observer of his age who also had visited the United States (his famous work, *Democracy in America,* was written as a result of that visit). While in Sicily, Tocqueville commented on the need especially to continue to make improvements and pursue innovations, in particular he recommended changes in the system of the *latifundia,* the large landed estates owned by the Sicilian nobility. Such changes, he believed, would benefit the economy overall.

It was during this time of economic growth that Sicily was moving inexorably toward the major event of modern Italian history—the *Risorgimento*—the resurgence of the Italian nation. As a result of the *Risorgimento,* during the second half of the 19th century, the island would finally be united with the rest of the nation. With that union, would come a new era in Sicily's own history and development.

XIII
The Risorgimento

THE LAST YEARS OF BOURBON RULE IN SICILY WERE A PERIOD OF POLITI-
cal turmoil and strife. In 1837, the new ideas of Italian independence
and unification, coupled with slow economic growth and the outbreak of cholera, touched off a series of revolts, especially in the
eastern part of the island. That year, at Catania, the yellow flag of
Sicily was raised in a protest for independence and a revolutionary
committee was formed. Rich and poor joined together in this revolt,
embracing each other in the streets and swearing allegiance to the
revolution. Although suppressed, it was a prelude to larger risings
that were to come.

The main causes of uprisings in Sicily were the general peasant
unrest and the widespread resentment of rule from Naples. There
was also a growing awareness that Sicily should be part of an independent Italy or perhaps part of a federation of Italian states. Ties
between Sicily and the mainland were growing and, even during the
years of Spanish rule, cultural contacts between the island and Italy
had never disappeared. Now, in the nineteenth century, they became
more and more important. Although the Sicilian dialect was used by
most people in day-to-day activities, Italian had become the written
language and also the *lingua franca* among Sicilians who might not be
familiar with each other's regional forms of speech. Italian had already become the language of government, and the major Italian
writers of the period, such as Ugo Foscolo and Alessandro Manzoni,
were now eagerly read on the island and Sicilian writers, such as
Giovanni Meli, in turn, became familiar to readers on the mainland.

In time, there would be, among Sicilians of various backgrounds,
an identification with the Italian movement for national unity, the
Risorgimento. One such early supporter in Sicily of the *Risorgimento*
was Michele Amari. A government official, he published a history of
the Sicilian Vespers which was actually a call for independence from

Bourbon rule. Amari went into exile in Paris and there met other Sicilian nationalists, including Francesco Crispi, who would one day become prime minister in the new united Italy, and Giuseppe La Farina an influential journalist. With others, these Sicilian nationalists taught themselves to be the kinds of political leaders that their homeland would need once liberated.

In 1848 revolution finally came. That whole year was one of revolt and revolution all over Europe. Among the first such uprisings was the one that took place in January at Palermo. Beginning at the University with student unrest, rioting spread to all parts of the city. Soon, a full scale revolution had broken out that quickly spread to other parts of the island. Many leaders and local heroes emerged during this revolt, and among the more colorful figures of the 1848 Sicilian revolution was the woman known as "Testa Di Lana." A goatherd who wore trousers and carried pistols, she (and her followers) fought the Bourbon police and militia throughout the island.

In a short time, the revolution had been successful and a provisional government was proclaimed, headed by the liberal leader Ruggiero Settimo. In July, this provisional government offered the crown of Sicily to a son of King Charles Albert of Piedmont, but he refused it in order not to antagonize Ferdinand II. Then, in September, a large Bourbon force landed at Messina and began to retake the island. Although the Sicilians were defeated, compromises were offered from Naples. It was however, too late. The spirit of the Risorgimento had come to Sicily and a growing movement for independence had captured the minds and hearts of the people. Moreover, the Sicilian revolution had also served to inspire risings all over the rest of Italy.

The events of 1848 were never forgotten by the Italians and eventually, in northern Italy, the Italian patriot Giuseppe Garibaldi, took up the idea of his compatriot, the leading Italian nationalist, Giuseppe Mazzini, to begin a new Sicilian rebellion that would become the basis for the unification of the Italian state. Already, the Sicilian patriot Crispi, who was a follower of Mazzini and Garibaldi, had returned to the island to popularize the nationalist program. Finally, an armed conflict at Palermo in April 1860 that turned into an insurrection provided the opportunity for Garibaldi to intervene.

Perhaps only a poet could do justice to the events of the next five months, such was this period of dramatic historical change. In May, Garibaldi arrived at the port of Marsala with his famous "Thousand Red Shirts," or *Camice Rosse,* a volunteer force that he had assembled to liberate the island. Their uniform, a red shirt, originated during one of Garibaldi's earlier campaigns in South America. Looking for a uniform for his soldiers in Montevideo, Uruguay, Garibaldi found a warehouse full of red shirts designed for use in slaughterhouses, and adapted them to his own use. The uniform came to symbolize both that legendary commander and his nationalist cause. Garibaldi was welcomed wherever he went and was greeted as a hero and even a saint who had come to redeem Sicily from centuries of foreign oppression. Next, at Salemi, Garibaldi proclaimed a dictatorship over Sicily in the name of King Victor Emmanuel of Piedmont. From Marsala, Garibaldi and his "Thousand" marched on to Salemi where they were joined by the Sicilian patriot and friar, Father Pantaleo. Soon the forces approached Calatafimi on the way to Palermo.

By now, Garibaldi's troops had been joined by many Sicilians including youths who were not yet even seventeen, the "picciotti," who would become part of the expeditionary force. Untrained and often poorly armed (any weapon that could be found was used, a musket, a scythe, an axe, even a nail at the end of a stick) this force, at Calatafimi, with the red-shirted Thousand leading the advance, had their first decisive victory over the Bourbon forces. Today, in that town, there stands a large monument commemorating the battle. It is inscribed with the famous word of Garibaldi, spoken just before the victory: "Here we will either make Italy or die." On the 27th of May, having broken through a Bourbon defense force of 25,000, the Red-shirts and the other volunteers entered Palermo. Fierce fighting began as, street by street, Garibaldi's volunteer forces took the city. After three days of fighting they were triumphant. An important hero of these events was the Sicilian, Giuseppe La Masa, who served as one of Garibaldi's commanders. He would later become a major general in the Italian army and a member of the new Italian parliament. A truce was arranged and Garibaldi proclaimed himself Dictator of the Two Sicilies, ruling in the name of King Victor Emmanuel of Italy. The citizens of the city immediately began pulling down the hated symbol of Bourbon rule, the Castellamare fortress, and Garibaldi was hailed as the liberator of the island. Full liberation was achieved on July 20, when the Garibaldini, who had been joined by thousands of Sicilians and volunteers from the north, won a victory against the Bourbon forces at Milazzo. Then, once Messina and Taormina were taken, Garibaldi, with a number of his men, boarded two steamships, the *Torino* and the *Franklin* and set out to cross the Straits. Partly through their efforts, a new and independent united Kingdom of Italy would soon be achieved of which

Sicily would be a part. All the world was stunned by the quick and decicisve victory of the Thousand and their companions in the Sicilian campaign. The success, of what appeared at first to many to be only a mad enterprise, was owed to Garibaldi. It was that commander who set the example of extreme bravery, who knew how to lead on the battlefield, and who inspired many, including such Italian patriots Sirtori, Bertani, Bixio, Mario, Crispi, Medici, and Depretis—all of whom shared military and political responsibility during their campaign with him. Also to be recognized is the courage, enthusiasm, and sacrifice of the Camice Rosse, the Redshirts, and the active and brave support of the many Sicilian patriots and soldiers. Italians felt a surge of pride as foreign admirers and supporters of the Italian cause appauded this achievement. The next step was to be the actual unification of the island with the rest of the nation.

In October 1860, a plebiscite was held in which a majority of 99.5 per cent favored unification with Italy under King Victor Emmanuel of Savoy. Unification with the rest of Italy would bring important changes. Sicily, for the first time in centuries, was not only free, but also had the advantage of joining a larger and more active market. And, although now subservient to the new national government, the Sicilian people at least now had more say in the destiny of their island.

Italian unification was finally completed in 1870 with the Italian army's occupation of Rome. In that year, the outbreak of the Franco-Prussian war forced the French troops, who had been there protecting the city for the Papacy, to return home. The Italian forces then occupied the city and proclaimed it the capital of Italy. Final unification of the nation meant, for all Italians, the start of a new era in their history and, especially for Sicily and her people, the prospect of a new beginning.

It should be noted that the decades following unification were, for Sicily, a period of important cultural achievements. At this time, many outstanding figures emerged in literature and the arts. Among writers and playwrights of the latter decades of the 19th and first decades of the 20th centuries, were the famous Nobel Prize winner, Luigi Pirandello (1867–1936), of Agrigento, who is probably best known for his drama *Six Characters in Search of an Author,* and Giovanni Verga (1840–1922), one of Italy's greatest novelists. Verga, whose works include *Cavalleria rusticana* (later made into an opera by Mascagni), was a native of Catania. In this context it is appropriate to mention the great composer, Vincenzo Bellini (1802–1835), born at Catania. Although he wrote during an earlier period, Bellini's glorious operas, which are still enjoyed the world over today and include the famous *Norma, La Sonnambula,* and *I Puritani,* were really popularized in the decades following unification.

During the post-unification period, important Sicilian political leaders also emerged. Among these were Francesco Crispi (1819–1901), who in 1887 became the first Sicilian to be named prime minister of Italy. He had been a disciple of the great patriot Mazzini and, before unification had been a leader in the struggle for Italian independence. Another significant political figure, Napoleone Colajanni (1847–1921) from Enna, had, like Crispi, been a follower of Mazzini and Garibaldi and later, as a leader in parliament, would initiate major reforms in Italian banking. Later, another Sicilian, Antonio di Rudinì (1839–1909), would also serve as an early prime minister. The pre-World War I foreign minister, Antonio di San Giuliano (1852–1914), was born in Catania, while the prime minister who led Italy through the First World War and was a central figure at the post-war Paris Peace Conference, Victor Emmanuel Orlando (1860–1952), was a native of Palermo.

Important Sicilian social leaders and reformers also emerged in at the decades immediately preceding and following the First World War. The Catanian journalist, Giuseppe De Felice-Giuffrida (1859–1920), was a founder of the *Fasci siciliani* movement (not to be confused with Mussolini's Fascism), that agitated in the post-unification period for land reform in Sicily. The *Fasci siciliani* were a network of industrial and agrarian workers' clubs that gave their name to the wave of popular unrest that had spread throughout the island in 1893–94. Starting as an industrial labor movement, the *fasci siciliani* soon became popular among the peasants and farmers of the countryside. The movement sponsored numerous political candidates and won several important local elections. A basis of its appeal was it platform demanded land reform, tax reductions, and local administrative reforms. Its popularity in the western part of the island can be attributed to the economic crisis that arose due to competition from foreign sulphur producers. Fear of the movement's strength became so great that, in 1893, Crispi decided to place the island under martial law. But his fears of violence and a possible separatist uprising ultimately proved to be unfounded.

In the area of social reform, the Sicilian priest, Don Luigi Sturzo (1871–1959), who was one of the most important Italian social thinkers of the first half of the twentieth century, must also be mentioned. Don Sturzo played an important role in checking the growth of the Communist party in Italy and was also an leading figure in the anti-fascist movement. And, one of the major Italian philosophers and political thinkers of the age, Gaetano Mosca (1858–1941), was also a Sicilian, born in Palermo. Mosca, whose works are still studied by political scientists and sociologists, eventually became a senator in the Italian parliament. From Caltanisetta in Sicily, came the other controversial philosopher and educator of the Fascist era, Giovanni Gentile (1875–1944). Gentile was one of the leading apologists of Mussolini's regime. In contrast, another Sicilian, Giuseppe Borghese (1882–1952) of Polizzi Generosa (near Palermo), a major literary critic and author, was one of the leading anti-fascists of the period. Later, he became professor of Romance languages at the University of Chicago.

But, although it was, in terms of cultural achievements, a most productive period, the post-unification era was, for many Italians, also a time of great economic hardship. Hundreds of thousands were forced to leave their homeland behind and immigrate to other parts of the world. Many, of course, came to America where they sought a better life for themselves and their families. In time, about one-fifth of the Italian immigrants to the U.S. would come from Sicily. From the ports of Messina and Palermo they boarded ships bound for American ports. In the U.S. they found jobs that, for Americans perhaps, were considered poorly paying ones, but not for these new immigrants. Wages of a dollar a day represented a *scudo*—a five lira piece—and that was an unheard of daily wage back home. In the inland communities of Sicily, many may never have even seen a *scudo*. In America, enough money could be earned to send some back home. At first, of course, the immigrants faced many hardships, but in time these were overcome. The rest is familiar history. Each generation advanced and helped to fulfill the dreams of those who first set out, often alone, from the ports of their island. They became successful as they helped to build the United States and the other countries to which they had immigrated. Through these efforts, they contributed greatly to the development of the world's modern economy.

Meanwhile, the decades of the 20th century meant, for Sicily, as they did for the rest of Italy, a time of war and political unrest. It was in the post-World War I era that Fascism would emerge and with it, the seeds of the Second World War. But, from out of that period of turmoil and difficulty, a modern Sicily would emerge and, with it, a new phase in the island's long, varied, and often turbulent, history would begin.

XIV
Modern Sicily

Soon after the end of World War I, Italy entered into the period of fascist rule. For Sicily, however, the history of the island under that regime is surprisingly brief. Mussolini for example, in his speeches and writings, paid less attention to the island than any previous prime minister did. And, although more money was now spent on public works, as was the case with the rest of Italy, there was still some resentment because the government also imposed more centralization and control from Rome.

Because the fascist regime wished to present the image of a powerful and problem-free nation to the rest of the world, it had to demonstrate that Italy's problems had already been solved. Thus those issues that faced Sicily and the rest of southern Italy would now simply be ignored. Even a journal entitled *The Problems of Sicily* had to change its name. Moreover, in an effort to "italianize" the culture, the names of towns in various parts of Italy were changed by Mussolini to more Italian or Roman sounding ones. In the case of Sicily this meant, for instance, that Girgenti became Agrigento, Terranova was changed back to Gela, Castrogiovanni was given its old name of Enna, and Piani dei Greci became Piana degli Albanesi.

In time, as Mussolini's policies became more extreme, signs of opposition appeared. Sicilian history, of course, had taught the people to be skeptical of any type of government and, a series of foreign wars after 1935, coupled with increased fascist challenges to traditional ways of life, helped to heighten this opposition. Orders for the compulsory surrender of agricultural products especially were met with widespread resistance while, more and more, other fascist policies were either ignored or disregarded. Despite all Mussolini's exhortations for a high national birth rate, for instance, the number of births in Sicily instead declined, and no amount of efforts by the fascists could prevent a widespread evasion of school by Sicilian children. Increasing interference with aspects of everyday life by the fascists, in dress (even professional people were supposed to wear uniforms), language, and behavior were all seen as annoyances and were generally unenforceable.

By 1940, there was widespread dissatisfaction, not only on the island, but throughout the rest of Italy, with the fascist regime. The nation was now involved in what would soon be a most unpopular war and, of course, by this point, all political dissent and opposition had been stifled. In Sicily, Mussolini tried to counter opposition by ordering all Sicilian-born officials transferred to the mainland because of suspected disloyalty. This was a most radical attempt to maintain political control. Although past rulers such as Charles of Anjou and Ferdinand II had themselves considered such a move, no ruler had ever gone so far as to implement it. It was, of course, met with great resistance and was never completely enforceable.

But the worst legacy of the regime was the war. Sicily, because of its insular nature, would naturally suffer hardships during any war, and especially one which had a Mediterranean front. Exports were curtained and sea travel to the mainland had to give priority to military traffic. Rationing was imposed, and the blackmarket flourished.

The island was, naturally, of strategic importance to both sides in the war, and soon the Allies chose it as the site for their first major invasion in Europe. In 1943, Allied forces landed near Gela. War had now come directly to Sicily and with it a great deal of destruction. Mussolini boasted that the island could never be taken and that his own forces would drive back the Allied invaders. This proved not to be true and, as he did not even dare to mobilize the local population for fear of a general uprising, the Allied advance through Sicily continued. The Americans swept through the western part of the island, while the British and Canadians fought German resistance in the east. As the invading forces moved on, they were generally welcomed by the people. An Allied victory meant the possibility of free government and even self-determination for the island. By 1944, Sicily was liberated and under Allied control.

The end of the war in 1945 left the island with a free government but also with widespread destruction to its economy and infrastructure. Dissatisfaction was again high and there was distrust of the new government. For a time, immediately following the war, the separatist question dominated Sicilian politics and there was some debate over the issue of a plebiscite to decide whether the island should become independent. A movement, the M.I.S. (Sicilian Independence Movement), and another group, the E.V.I.S. (Voluntary Army of Sicilian Independence) were even planning armed risings to achieve political independence or the creation of an autonomous state. A petition regarding these issues was addressed to the San Francisco Peace Conference and there was even some talk about annexation of the island to the United States.

To solve this dilemma, and to address the separatist feelings that were so strong in this early post-war period, the new Italian government, in 1946, granted a large measure of autonomy to Sicily. It was felt that a new period had begun, both for the now autonomous island and for the newly formed Italian Republic. For Sicily, autonomy meant that there would be a regional parliament that could give more attention to local affairs and problems. In time, regional autonomy, or self-government, would be granted to other areas of Italy.

For Sicily, the post-war period also meant a time of renewed economic activity. Improvements in agriculture were initiated; citrus growing, for example, was greatly improved and grain production increased. In industry, the use of electrical power rose ten times beyond its pre-war level and a large electrical cable was extended over the Straits of Messina to bring power from the mainland. But, it was the discovery of oil that was perhaps the most surprising post-war development. In 1953, the Gulf Oil Company struck oil near Ragusa and production was soon begun. The Italian company ENI discovered another field off the coast of Gela, and Sicily shortly became responsible for most of the production of the entire Italian oil industry. A refinery was built near the port of Augusta that, by 1966, was refining over eight million tons of crude oil per year. Meanwhile, methane gas was discovered near Gagliano and at Bronte, while discoveries of large potash deposits were being made elsewhere on the island. It should be noted again that these discoveries were especially important, because Sicilian sulphur production, which at one time had accounted for almost half the island's exports, had earlier in this century been severely undercut by U.S. competition. Newly discovered deposits in Louisiana and an improved process of extraction, had made American sulphur available at under the cost price of the Sicilian product.

In the post-World War II period, the discovery and development of new sources of power and energy continued to have great effects on the Sicilian economy. Because of this, vast improvements and changes are today in evidence everywhere. The town of Gela, for instance, changed more in five years than it had in the previous thousand, and the southern coast of the island now had an important port for the first time. On the east coast, the city of Augusta emerged as the largest and busiest Sicilian harbor, and by the 1960's it was second only to Genoa as the foremost Italian port. And Syracuse, after many centuries, was again becoming the dynamic area it had been in antiquity. A new Sicily had emerged, replacing the historic Sicily of previous centuries.

The second half of this century also saw a new generation of Sicilian scholars, artists, writers, and administrators, all of whom would contribute to the island's modern cultural development. The novelist and playwright Vitaliano Brancati (1907–1954), for example, wrote in his works of the dilemmas of the fascist and post-war periods, and the poet Lucio Piccolo (1903–1969), the cousin of the famous author of *The Leopard,* Tomasi di Lampedusa (1896–1957), fixed in poetry a description of the unique Sicilian world. Lampedusa, of course, had written one of the greatest novels of the twentieth century, evoking in *The Leopard* (published 1958), the transition on his island between the old order and the new. Likewise, Elio Vittorini (1908–1966), who was born in Syracuse, would also achieve fame as a noted novelist. His works include *Le donne di Messina* and *Garofano rosso*. One of Italy's greatest modern poets and Nobel Prize winner, Salvatore Quasimodo (1901–1968), from Modica, in his work bridged the gap between classical poetry and modern, and the novelist Leonardo Sciascia, from Agrigento, has been described as Sicily's finest living writer. Other outstanding twentieth century Sicilians include Stanislao Cannizzaro, who was among the first to understand the true structure of the atom, and Ettore Majorana, a prophet of nuclear fission. Among post-war political leaders and administrators are Mario Scelba who, inspired by the writings of Luigi Sturzo, was one of the founders of the Christian Democratic Party, and Ugo La Malfa who led the Italian Republican Party.

Tourism is also an important part of modern Sicily, and the island can be considered a paradise for both vacationers and students of history alike. Making a circuit of the cities from Palermo to Messina to Syracuse and back again, one can see the fascinating mixture of old and new. Where else, in only a week or ten days, can one see the results of so many diverse cultures over so many centuries? All over the island are fine hotels, ranging from the comfortable to the deluxe. Beautiful beaches are, of course, everywhere.

Finally, a word must be said about the tempting and varied cuisine of the island. Sicily, with it nine regions, is considered by many to have the most diverse cuisine of all of Italy. A visit to the markets of any Sicilian town reveals variety of products that made such a city as Syracuse, for example, the gastronomic capital of the ancient world. Everywhere on the island are famous seafood dishes, with Messina, especially offering many unique restaurants featuring such a menu. The influence of many cultures is also apparent in the cuisine. The Saracen influence on the island is evident in such specialties as *pasta con le sarde,* a pasta dish featuring sardines that traditionally was invented to feed the Saracen troops as they landed to conquer the island. Trapani offers the Arab-inspired couscous. And, of course, the ever present citrus fruits, that also form parts of many recipes, as well as many vegetables such as eggplant, are also part of the Arabic heritage. The Spanish contributed too, bringing the *frittata,* a type of tortilla or omelette, flavored with artichoke or wild asparagus. Inspired by more recent history, the city of Catania offers *pasta alla Norma,* named in honor of the famous opera composed by that city's native son, Bellini. Then, there are the many desserts, such as *cannoli,* featuring the cheeses of the island, and the ubiquitous and delicious sherbets and ices, a specialty since early conquerors first used the snows of Mount Etna to cool their after-dinner sweets.

In all aspects of its culture and life, the history of the island is vividly present, and offers fascination and the possibility of new discoveries to everyone. It was Goethe who wrote, "Italy without Sicily leaves no clear impression on the human mind: Sicily is the key to it all." Being at the center of the Mediterranean, with its thousands of years of history and civilization, Sicily, draws both the tourist and the scholar, to explore the living traces of its most unique, varied, and fascinating history.

Time Line

Sicily	Elsewhere
c. 20,000 B.C. Cave paintings Egadi Islands	Paleolithic period cave paintings, Lescaux, etc.
c. 3,000 B.C. Stentinello culture, use of copper, "Sesi" built, agriculture begins on Sicily	Neolithic period beginning of agriculture in the Mediterranean area
c. 1200 B.C. Sicani, Sicels, Elmyrians arrive on Sicily	Bronze Age, period of the Trojan War
c. 800 B.C. Greeks first explore Sicily	rise of the Greek polis; Carthage founded
c. 650 B.C. Greek colonies established in Sicily	City-states in Greece
c. 575 B.C. Greek temples built in Sicily; rise of the tyrants	Tyrants in Athens and other Greek cities
c. 480 B.C. rule of Gelon	The Persian War; beginning of the classical Age
c. 425 B.C. Athenian expedition to Sicily	Peloponnesian War
c. 360 B.C. rule of Dionysos of Syracuse	Age of Socrates, Plato, Aristotle

c. 325 B.C. rule of Agathocles	Rise of Alexander the Great, the Hellenistic Age
c. 250 B.C. Romans arrive in Sicily	First Punic War
c. 210 B.C. Sicily a base for Roman military operations	Second Punic War, Hannibal invades Italy
c. 145 B.C. Roman rule consolidated in Sicily	Third Punic War, defeat of Carthage
c. 130 B.C. slave revolts	Gracchi revolt in Rome
c. 50–1 B.C. "Pax Romana" comes to Sicily	Age of Caesar and Augustus, the Empire begins
c. 100–300 A.D. Sicily a peaceful Roman Province; Christianity appears	Roman Empire at its height
c. 450 Various barbarian tribes invade Sicily	Invasions of the Western Roman Empire, Dark Ages begin
c. 550–800 Byzantines in Sicily	Rise of the Byzantine Empire
c. 850–900 Arab conquest of Sicily; introduction of new crops	Arab invasions of Europe; Empire of Charlemagne
c. 1060–1190 Norman invasion of Sicily (1061), rule of Norman kings (Roger, William, etc.), the Golden Age, cathedrals of Palermo, Monreale, & Cefalù	Norman invasion of England (1066); the Romanesque style; the Crusades
c. 1190–1210 Henry VI takes Sicily; King Frederick's court at Palermo, Sicilian School of Poetry	Papacy at its height under Innocent III

c. 1210 King Frederick's court at Palermo, Sicilian School of Poetry	Magna Carta (1215); the Troubadours; Franciscan order established
c. 1270 Sicily taken by Charles of Anjou	Thomas Aquinas; Gothic Age in art
c. 1280–85 Sicilian Vespers end of Angevin rule	Edward I of England conquers Wales; Hapsburgs secure Holy Roman Empire
c. 1290–1350 reign of Peter of Aragon	Model Parliament in England; Dante writing in Italy
c. 1350–1450 rule of Aragon; Sicilian cities extend their trade in the Mediterranean	Humanism begins; Bubonic Plague; Jacquerie revolt in France
c. 1450–1525 uprisings on Sicily, protests of Sicilian Parliament against Spanish viceroys; Renaissance	Period of the Renaissance and Reformation; Peasant revolt in Germany; Turkish conquest of Constantinople; Columbus reaches New World
c. 1525–1650 Spanish rule in in Sicily; rise in Sicilian population	Colonial Empires built; Civil war in England; Louis XIV in France; Thirty Years War
c. 1650–1700 Eruption of Mt. Etna—rebuilding of Noto and Catania in Baroque style; Rocco Pirri historian; Pietro Novelli painter	Baroque age in art; Scientific rev.—Newton, Galeleo, etc; Peter the Great in Russia
c. 1700–1750 Victor Amadeus, king; Battle of Francavilla, Austrian rule; Sicilian Enlightenment, University of Palermo est.	Maria Theresa in Austria; Louis XV in France; the Enlightenment, Locke, Voltaire, Diderot, etc

c. 1750–1800 Goethe visits Sicily; reforms of Carraciolo; Bourbon rule; ideas of French Rev. come to Sicily

The American and French Revolutions; Romantic age in the arts begins

c. 1800–1850 British in Sicily; Industrial Revolution; Bellini composes his operas

Napoleonic Wars; Peace of 1815; Industrial Rev.

c. 1850–1900 Risorgimento, Garibaldi takes Sicily; Crispi, De Felice in politics; Pirandello in drama; emigration begins

The Risorgimento; Unification of Germany; Franco-Prussian War; U.S. Civil War

c. 1900–1945 emigration continues; Orlando, di Rudini in politics; fascism & W.W. II come to Sicily

World War I; rise of the dictatorships; World War II

c. 1945–present Autonomy for Sicily, oil discovered near Ragusa; Quasimodo, Lampedusa, etc. in the arts

Italian Republic established "Economic Miracle" in Italy; end of the colonial age; the "cold war;" atomic age

APPENDIX B

What Places to See in Sicily—A Circuit Tour of the Island

A FINE WAY TO SEE SICILY IS BY CAR. THERE ARE EXCELLENT HIGHWAYS as well as modern and comfortable hotels everywhere. The route would be a circuitous one, starting at Messina, proceeding west to Palermo, then south to Trapani and finally east to Syracuse and Catania. It would finish at Taormina before coming back to Messina. Many other interesting stops can be made along the way. The tour-route is as follows:

Start by seeing Messina itself. Sight in that city include the famous Cathedral with its high campanile, a bell-tower that has a the famous and elaborate astronomical clock with its animated figures. The public gardens and the Museo Nazionale are also noteworthy, the latter containing many paintings rescued from the 1908 earthquake. Then, leaving the city, proceed west, passing the Gola dell'Alcantara, a beautiful natural gorge. On the way there is a magnificent view of Mt. Etna.

The route west to Palermo continues on the S.S. 113 highway and passes through Tindari, the ancient Tyndaris, last of the Greek colonies founded in Sicily.

Then, arrive at Cefalù, a beautiful port which has retained much of its character and charm. In the Piazza del Duomo is the cathedral, one of the finest buildings of the Norman period. It was built by King Roger who, when shipwrecked, vowed to build a church wherever he came safely ashore. Beyond Cefalù follow the A 19 highway to see the ruins of Soluntum, an ancient Phoenician settlement that later was also a Roman town.

Now, on to Palermo. The sights of Palermo, which rests amidst the beautiful plain of the Conca d'Ora, are many. The city's cathedral and Norman Palace are the among the world's most outstanding examples of Norman art and are certainly worth a visit. The interesting church of S. Giovanni with its curious Saracenic domes can be seen nearby. While in the city one must also visit the *Vucciria,* the colorful market-place and sample the specialties of the region. A side trip should, of course, be taken to visit Monreale and its famous cathedral and cloister, in Norman, Saracen, and Romanesque style. Of particular note are the magnificent mosaics.

South from Monreale is the site of the ancient city of Segesta, one of the oldest towns in Sicily, being founded by the island's earliest inhabitants, the Elymians. There is a Greek temple of the 5th century B.C., one of the best preserved on the island. And, just three km. beyond is Calatafimi, a castle town with the monument erected to commemorate Garibaldi's victory there in 1860.

Traveling south, the next part of the circuit begins in Trapani. The sights at Trapani, which is situated on a sickle-shaped peninsula, include the cathedral and the old harbor town. An excursion can be made from here to Erice (the ancient Eryx) which in antiquity was the site of a much venerated shrine to the goddess Aphrodite. From Trapani, the Egadi islands, site of prehistoric Sicilian artifacts and structures, can also be reached. And, a short distance south from Trapani, on the mainland, brings one to the Phoenician ruins at Mozia. There, one can find some of the best and most fascinating remains of that ancient Mediterranean culture.

Then, southward on the next part of the circuit. On the way, one stops at Marsala, where the major attractions would include visits to the various wine making establishments, especially the Woodhouse and Florio firms. The city also has a fine cathedral dedicated to St. Thomas of Canterbury, and there are some Roman ruins, including some houses and public baths.

Traveling southeast on S.S. 115, one comes to Solinunte, one of the most interesting sites on the island. Its ancient Greek ruins include an acropolis, temples, and the old wall of the city. Some of the temples there are among the largest of the ancient Greek world.

From Solinunte one travels further east to Agrigento, the road to the

120

city itself passing between two ancient Greek temples. The Greek temples are, in fact, a major attraction of the place, which also has a fine archaeologic museum. It is at Agrigento that the temples can best be seen in February, when they are framed by the new almond blossoms. A festival takes place there every year at that time.

Then, on to Gela, which is one of Sicily's principal ports, is a seaside resort, and also has some interesting Greek ruins. Continuing on east from Gela on S.S. 115, one comes to the city of Ragusa, with its beautiful baroque churches and Roman and pre-Roman ruins. Further on, to the east, is Noto which, because of the earthquake of 1693, was completely rebuilt as a grand baroque city. It has several churches and palaces done in that magnificent 17th century style that are worth seeing.

From Noto, one continues on northeast to Syracuse, one of the oldest and most fascinating cities of Sicily. The old town with its narrow, winding streets, the Greek and Roman ruins, the ancient temples and amphitheatres, and sights such as the Fountain of Arethusa, and the "Ear of Dionysos," make it a most noteworthy stop on the circuit tour of the island. In the Greek theaters one can still attend performances of Greek plays, while the Catacombs, larger than those even of Rome, and other diverse sights from different historic periods make Syracuse a microcosm of Sicilian history.

From Syracuse, one starts on the last part of the circuit tour, towards Taormina. Traveling north on S.S. 114 one comes first to Catania, site of a university and Sicily's second largest city. Rebuilt after the 1693 earthquake, Catania is also a beautiful baroque city, but also contains several important ancient sights, such as the Odeon, or Roman theater. The most rewarding excursion out from Catania is to Mt. Etna. Italy's highest mountain after the Alpine peaks, Mt. Etna is also an active volcano, the mouth of which can be reached by cablecar and a 45 minute walk. The trip to see the top is well worth it, passing first through olive and citrus groves, then mountain pine, the snow line, and the blackened top that glistens in the sun.

North from Catania, one travels on to Taormina, completing the circuit tour of the island. Picturesque Taormina, with is many gardens, vistas, and charming hotels, is claimed by many to be the most beautiful place in all of Sicily. It is an ideal resort. From the top of its Greek theater is one of the best views of Mt. Etna, in both the morning and afternoon light. It is no wonder that the poets have been inspired by this site to sing the praises of all Sicily.

There are, of course, many other sights and places throughout the island that can be reached by short excursions and detours from this main circuit tour. With modern and well-signed motorways pointing the way and the use of a roadmap, one can easily follow the circuitous route and see all the sights mentioned, and more. It is a tour of more than five thousand years of history that can be accomplished with enjoyment and ease.

Index

124